1

The ABCs of Artificial Intelligence

"Things You Need to Know!"

Kelly Emrick MBA, Ph.D.

Dedication

To all those who seek understanding in an increasingly complex world, may this book shed light on the transformative power of artificial intelligence, its implications for our society, and our role in its evolution.

Table of Contents

Chapter 4: The Ethical and Societal Implications of AI (Page 38)

- AI in governance: Surveillance, crime prevention, and public services

- The social and economic implications of AI

Chapter 5: AI Ethics - The Debate on AI and Humanity (Page 42)

- The moral and ethical considerations of AI

- The debate over AI rights and responsibilities

- AI bias and fairness

- The role of regulation in AI development

Chapter 6: The Future of AI - Possibilities, Predictions, and Preparations (Page 46)

- Future applications of AI: From climate change to space exploration

- Predictions for the future of AI: The optimists and the pessimists

- The societal impact of advanced AI: Job displacement and new opportunities

- Preparing for an AI-driven future: Education and policy recommendations

Chapter 7: AI and Data - The Fuel of the Future (Page 50)

- Understanding the role of data in AI

- Big data and its implications for AI development

- The importance of data privacy and security in AI

Chapter 8: The Role of AI in Cybersecurity (Page 54)

- AI in cyber defense: anomaly detection, threat prediction, and response

- AI in cyber offense: the rise of AI-powered cyber attacks

Chapter 9: AI and Healthcare - Saving Lives with Algorithms (Page 57)

- AI in diagnostics, treatment, and patient care

- The future of AI in healthcare: personalized medicine, AI surgeons, and more

- Ethical considerations in AI healthcare

Chapter 10: AI and the Environment - A Double-Edged Sword (Page 61)

- The role of AI in combating climate change and promoting sustainability

- The environmental footprint of AI: energy use and e-waste

- Future prospects for green AI

Chapter 11: AI and Entertainment - The Changing Face of Media (Page 65)

- AI in video games, movies, and music

- The rise of AI influencers and digital artists

- The future of entertainment in an AI-driven world

Chapter 12: AI and the Job Market - Opportunities and Threats (Page 70)

- The impact of AI on job displacement and creation

- The changing nature of work in an AI-driven world

- Preparing the workforce for AI: education and training

Chapter 13: AI Governance - The Need for Oversight and Regulation (Page 73)

- The current state of AI governance and regulation

- The challenges and considerations in creating AI policy

- Case studies of AI governance around the world

Chapter 14: AI and Global Politics - The New Arms Race (Page 76)

- The role of AI in military and defense

- AI as a factor in global power dynamics

- The ethics and implications of autonomous weapons

Chapter 15: AI and Education - The Future of Learning (Page 83)

- How AI is transforming teaching and learning

- The role of AI in personalized education

- The challenges and opportunities of AI in education

Chapter 16: AI and Finance - Algorithms on Wall Street (Page 90)

- The use of AI in banking and financial services

- How AI is shaping the future of trading and investment

- The implications of AI in financial regulation and security

Chapter 25: The Philosophy of AI - Consciousness, Rights, and Existential Questions (Page 129)

- The debate on AI consciousness and personhood
- The potential rights and responsibilities of AI entities

Chapter 26: AI and Retail - Revolutionizing the Shopping Experience (Page 133)

- The use of AI in personalizing customer experience
- How AI is transforming retail operations and logistics
- The future of retail in an AI-driven world

Chapter 27: AI and Real Estate - Building Smarter Cities (Page 138)

- The role of AI in property valuation and investment
- How AI is shaping urban planning and architecture
- The implications of AI in real estate and housing

Chapter 28: AI and Manufacturing - Automating the Factory Floor (Page 142)

- The use of AI in production automation and quality control
- The impact of AI on supply chain management
- The future of manufacturing in an AI-driven world

Chapter 29: AI and Tourism - Traveling with Algorithms (Page 146)

- The role of AI in personalized travel recommendations

Chapter 34: AI and Archaeology - Unearthing the Past with Algorithms (Page 168)

- The use of AI in archaeological analysis and preservation
- How AI is changing the way we understand history
- The future of archaeology in an AI-driven world

Chapter 35: AI and Music - The Symphony of Algorithms (Page 172)

- The role of AI in music composition and production
- The implications of AI in the music industry
- The future of music in an AI-driven world

Chapter 36: AI and Religion - Faith in Algorithms (Page 176)

- The role of AI in religious practices and theological reflections
- The ethical and societal implications of AI in religion
- The future of religion in an AI-driven world

Chapter 37: AI and Gaming - Playing with Algorithms (Page 180)

- The role of AI in game design and player interactions
- How AI is changing the landscape of the gaming industry
- The future of gaming in an AI-driven world

Chapter 38: AI and Insurance - Predicting the Future (Page 184)

- The use of AI in risk assessment and policy pricing

- How AI is transforming the insurance industry

- The future of insurance in an AI-driven world

Chapter 39: AI and the Human Body - Augmenting our Capabilities (Page 188)

- The role of AI in personal health tracking and body augmentation

- The ethical and societal implications of AI in body augmentation

- The future of human body in an AI-driven world

Chapter 40: AI and the Animal Kingdom - Understanding our Fellow Inhabitants (195)

- The use of AI in animal behavior studies and conservation efforts

- The implications of AI in our understanding of the animal kingdom

- The future of animal studies in an AI-driven world

Afterword: The ABCs of AI - A Recap and Reflection (Page 199)

- Reflecting on the journey of understanding AI

- Revisiting the ABCs of AI

- Final thoughts on the transformative potential of AI and its implications for the future of our world

- Existential questions and concerns raised by AI

Conclusion: Living with AI - Adapting to a New Normal (Page 203)

- Embracing the AI Revolution

- The importance of understanding and engaging with AI

- The role of individuals, governments, and organizations in shaping AI's future

- Final thoughts on the journey of AI and its impact on society

- Reflecting on the pervasive impact of AI in every facet of life

- How to adapt to a world increasingly driven by AI

- A call to action for responsible AI use and advocacy

Glossary: Understanding AI Jargon (Page 207)

- Definitions of key AI terms and phrases for easy reference

Epilogue: The Journey from Dawn to Adaptation - An AI Odyssey (Page 210)

Introduction

The Dawn of Artificial Intelligence

Artificial Intelligence (AI) is rooted in the assumption that human thought can be mechanized. The concept of formal or mechanical reasoning has a long history, with contributions from philosophers who developed structured methods of formal deduction in the first millennium BCE. Their ideas were further developed over the centuries by philosophers such as Aristotle, Euclid, al-Khwārizmī, and European scholastic philosophers. Notably, the 17th-century philosophers Leibniz, Thomas Hobbes, and René Descartes explored the possibility that all rational thought could be made as systematic as algebra or geometry, leading to the physical symbol system hypothesis that would become a guiding principle in AI research.

In the 20th century, the study of mathematical logic laid the groundwork that made AI seem plausible. This was established by works such as Boole's The Laws of Thought and Frege's Begriffsschrift. The answer to David Hilbert's fundamental question, "can all of mathematical reasoning be formalized?" was provided by Gödel's incompleteness proof, Turing's machine, and Church's Lambda calculus. Their work suggested that, within certain limits, any form of mathematical reasoning could be mechanized, leading to the Church-Turing thesis that a mechanical device could imitate any conceivable process of mathematical deduction. A key insight into AI came with the invention of the Turing machine, a theoretical construct that encapsulated the essence of abstract symbol manipulation.

From Turing's Machine to the First AI Programs: The Birth of AI

The roots of AI can be traced back to classical philosophers who attempted to describe human thinking as a symbolic system. Nevertheless, the real birth of AI as a science field began with the digital computer's development. During World War II, British mathematician and logician Alan Turing played a pivotal role in breaking the German Enigma code, leading to Allied victories against Nazi Germany. Turing developed the concept of a universal machine (later called the Turing machine) capable of computing anything computable. The central concept of the modern computer was based on Turing's ideas.

In 1950, Turing published a paper titled "Computing Machinery and Intelligence," where he proposed a test, now known as the Turing Test, to evaluate a machine's ability to exhibit intelligent behavior equivalent to, or indistinguishable from, that of a human. The Turing Test essentially assesses whether a machine can "think." The field of AI as we know it began to take shape in the mid-20th century with the creation of the Logic Theorist, the first program deliberately engineered to perform automated reasoning, often described as "the first artificial intelligence program." Logic Theorist was developed in 1956 by Allen Newell, Herbert A. Simon, and Cliff Shaw, and it proved 38 of the first 52 theorems in Whitehead and Russell's Principia Mathematica. Some theorems were even proved in new and more elegant ways than the originals.

The creation of the Logic Theorist was an outcome of key insights by Newell and Simon. Simon, a political scientist studying bureaucracies and decision-making, saw a printer typing out a map at RAND Corporation and realized that a machine manipulating symbols could simulate decision-making and possibly the process of human thought. Newell, studying logistics and organization theory, was inspired by Oliver Selfridge's work on pattern matching, leading him to understand how the interaction of simple, programmable units could accomplish complex behavior, including intelligent human behavior.

The first version of the Logic Theorist was hand-simulated, with program components distributed across 3x5 cards. The program successfully proved theorems, demonstrating that it could perform at the level of a talented mathematician. The term "artificial intelligence" was coined by John McCarthy during the summer of 1956 when he and Marvin Minsky,

Claude Shannon, and Nathan Rochester organized a conference on the subject. During this conference, Newell and Simon presented the Logic Theorist, marking a significant milestone in the development of AI.

While the Logic Theorist is considered the first AI program, many other early AI programs contributed to the field. One notable example is chess-playing computer programs, which became a standard for AI capability and a test bed for AI techniques, giving the field a psychological boost. Additionally, the development of AI planning, a branch of AI that involves decision-making tasks, also significantly contributed to the field, particularly with Shakey the robot, the first general-purpose mobile robot to reason about its actions.

This is a high-level overview of artificial intelligence's birth and early development. As AI evolves, it builds on these foundational concepts and breakthroughs to create more complex and capable systems.

The Touring Test Explained

The Turing Test estimates a machine's ability to exhibit intelligent behavior equivalent to or indistinguishable from a human. The test was introduced by Alan Turing in his 1950 paper, "Computing Machinery and Intelligence."

The Turing Test is a natural conversation between a human evaluator and two other parties: humans and machines designed to generate human-like responses. The evaluator is aware that one of the two partners in conversation is a machine, and all participants are separated. If the evaluator cannot reliably tell the machine from the human (Turing originally suggested that the machine would convince a human 30% of the time after five minutes of conversation), the machine is said to have passed the test.

The Turing Test is not without its critics. Some argue that it is too anthropocentric, meaning that it is biased toward human intelligence. Others argue that the test is too easy to game and that machines can be programmed to pass the test without being intelligent.

Despite its critics, the Turing Test remains an important milestone in the development of artificial intelligence. It has helped legitimize AI research and inspired the development of more sophisticated AI systems. Here are some of the major milestones in AI development:

- 1950: Alan Turing proposes the Turing Test.
- 1956: The Dartmouth Summer Research Project on Artificial Intelligence is held, which is considered the beginning of the field of AI research.
- 1966: Joseph Weizenbaum creates ELIZA, a program that can simulate a Rogerian psychotherapist.
- 1969: John McCarthy coins the term "expert system."
- 1972: Edward Feigenbaum and his team at Stanford University create Dendral, the first expert system for predicting the structure of organic molecules.
- 1981: The first chess program to beat a grandmaster is developed by IBM.
- 1997: IBM's Deep Blue computer defeats world chess champion, Garry Kasparov.
- 2011: Watson, a computer developed by IBM, wins the Jeopardy! Quiz show.
- 2016: AlphaGo, a computer program developed by Google DeepMind, defeats Lee Sedol, a professional Go player.
- 2023: OpenAI, Microsoft, and Google release large language modules (LLM) based on billions of neural connections to make intelligent predictive assessments.

These are just a few of the many milestones in the development of AI. As AI research progresses, we will likely see even more amazing advances.

Prelude

Large Language Models and Neural Networks

Artificial Intelligence (AI), once a concept found only in science fiction, has become a reality. It is transforming industries, revolutionizing technology, and increasingly integrating into our everyday lives. One of the most potent manifestations of AI is large language models (LLMs), capable of generating human-like text and understanding language in a way unimaginable just a few years ago.

At the heart of these models are neural networks, biologically inspired computing systems that mirror the structure of neurons in the human brain. Neural networks consist of interconnected nodes, or "neurons," arranged in layers. Each neuron takes in input, processes it (often nonlinearly), and passes it on to the next layer. In addition, neural networks can "learn" from experience, adjusting the weights that determine each input's importance through a training process.

Training a neural network involves feeding it a large amount of data and using a method called backpropagation to adjust the network weights. Backpropagation is essentially a way of attributing error to each neuron in the network so that it can adjust its weights to minimize that error in future predictions. This learning process is supervised, meaning the network is provided with correct answers during training to guide its learning.

Deep learning is a subfield of AI focusing on neural networks with many layers - hence "deep." These deep neural networks have shown remarkable ability in many tasks, such as image recognition and natural language processing, due to their capacity to model complex patterns and structures.

Large language models, such as GPT-3 by OpenAI, are examples of deep learning. They consist of an architecture called Transformer, which is particularly well-suited for understanding the context of language tasks. For example, transformers use a mechanism called attention to weighing the importance of different words in a sentence when making predictions. This allows them to generate highly coherent and contextually appropriate responses, making them seem almost human-like in their language understanding.

However, while LLMs like GPT-3 are impressive, they have limitations. They do not understand text in the way humans do. Instead, they identify and reproduce patterns in the data they were trained on. This means that while they can generate plausible-sounding responses, they do not truly comprehend the meaning behind the text.

Moreover, LLMs are sensitive to input phrasing and can produce different outputs for slight rephrases of the same prompt. They can also write plausible-sounding but incorrect or nonsensical answers. Finally, regarding ethical considerations, LLMs can potentially generate harmful or biased content, as they can reproduce biases in the data they were trained on. Despite these challenges, developing LLMs and neural networks represents a significant step forward in AI. These technologies' potential applications and impacts are vast as we refine these models and develop new techniques to mitigate their limitations. From virtual assistants to content generation and translation services to tutoring systems, the possibilities are limited only by our imagination. This is the dawn of a new era in artificial intelligence. As we stand at the forefront of this technological revolution, we must understand the mechanics that drive these systems, their potential, and the challenges we must overcome.

Chapter 1: The Evolution of AI - A Journey from Turing to Today

The concept of artificial intelligence (AI) has been around for centuries, but it was not until the mid-20th century that the field of AI research began to take off. One of the key figures in the early days of AI research was Alan Turing, a British mathematician considered the father of AI. In 1950, Turing published a paper titled "Computing Machinery and Intelligence," he proposed the Turing Test, a test of a machine's ability to exhibit intelligent behavior equivalent to, or indistinguishable from, that of a human. The Turing Test was a major milestone in the development of AI, and it helped to legitimize the field of AI research. In the years following the publication of Turing's paper, AI research made significant progress, and several early AI systems were developed. These systems could perform various tasks, including playing chess, translating languages, and diagnosing diseases.

However, the early AI systems were limited in their capabilities. They were often brittle, meaning small input data changes could easily fool them. They were also inefficient, requiring much time and computing power to perform simple tasks. In the 1980s, AI research entered a decline known as the "AI winter." This was due to several factors, including the failure of some high-profile AI projects and the lack of progress in developing more efficient AI algorithms. AI research regained interest in the 1990s, thanks partly to the development of new AI algorithms, such as neural networks. Neural networks are inspired by how the human brain works and are very effective at learning from data. In recent years, AI research has made even more progress, thanks to the development of new technologies, such as big data and cloud computing. These technologies have enabled training AI systems on much larger datasets, leading to significant performance improvements. As a result of these advances, AI is now being used in a wide variety of applications, including:

- Self-driving cars
- Virtual assistants
- Medical diagnosis
- Financial trading
- Fraud detection
- Content moderation

The impact of AI on Society and Industries so Far

AI has already had a significant impact on society and industries. For example, several companies, including Google, Uber, and Tesla, are developing self-driving cars. These cars have the potential to revolutionize transportation, making it safer, more efficient, and more accessible. Virtual assistants like Amazon Alexa and Apple Siri are also becoming increasingly popular. These assistants can control smart home devices, get information, and set reminders. AI is also used in the medical field to diagnose diseases, develop new treatments, and personalized care. For example, AI algorithms analyze medical images, such as X-rays and MRI scans, to identify potential problems.

In the financial industry, AI trades stocks predicts market trends, and detects fraud. For example, AI algorithms analyze large amounts of financial data to identify patterns that could indicate a stock is about to rise or fall in price. AI is also being used to moderate content on social media platforms. For example, AI algorithms identify and remove hate speech, terrorist propaganda, and other harmful content. AI's impact will only grow in the years to come. As AI algorithms become more powerful and efficient, they can be used to solve even more complex problems. As a result, AI has the potential to revolutionize many industries and significantly impact society.

Chapter 2: The Mechanics of AI - Simplified

Artificial intelligence (AI) is a branch of computer science that deals with creating intelligent agents, systems that can reason, learn, and act autonomously. AI research has successfully developed effective techniques for solving various problems, from game playing to medical diagnosis. The mechanics of AI are based on the following principles:

- Data: AI systems learn from data. The more data they have, the better they can perform.
- Algorithms: AI systems use algorithms to process data and make decisions. Algorithms are instructions that tell the computer how to solve a problem.

- Computation: AI systems use computation to process data and make decisions. Computation is the process of carrying out mathematical operations on data.

These principles are used to build AI systems that can perform various tasks. For example, AI systems can be used to:

- Play games
- Diagnose diseases
- Translate languages
- Write creative content
- Drive cars
- Perform complex mathematical computations
- Generate AI-based images

AI research continues progressing at compounding rates, and AI systems will continue to become even more powerful and capable. As a result, AI systems will eventually be able to perform tasks currently considered to be the exclusive domain of humans.

Basic principles of AI: Machine Learning and Deep Learning

Machine learning is a type of AI that allows systems to learn without being explicitly programmed. Instead, machine learning systems are trained on data and use that data to learn how to perform a task. For example, a machine learning system could be trained on a dataset of images of cats and dogs. After training, the system could identify cats and dogs in new images.

Deep learning is a type of machine learning that uses artificial neural networks to learn. Artificial neural networks are inspired by the way the human brain works. They are made up of interconnected nodes, and they learn by adjusting the strength of the connections between the nodes. Deep learning systems have succeeded in various tasks, such as image recognition, natural language processing, image generation, and speech recognition.

The Building Blocks of AI: Data, Algorithms, and Computation

The building blocks of AI are data, algorithms, and computation. Data is used to train AI systems. Algorithms are used to process data and make decisions. Finally, computation is used to carry out mathematical operations on data.

- Data is the most important building block of AI. AI systems can only learn and perform tasks if they can access data. The more data an AI system has, the better it can perform.
- Algorithms are the second most important building block of AI. Algorithms are used to process data and make decisions. There are many different types of algorithms, and each type is used for a different purpose. For example, some algorithms are used to classify data, while others are used to predict outcomes.
- Computation is the third most important building block of AI. Computation is used to carry out mathematical operations on data. Computation is needed to train AI systems and to make them perform tasks.

Types of AI: Narrow AI, General AI, and Superintelligent AI

- Narrow AI: A type of AI that is designed to perform a specific task. For example, a narrow AI system could be designed to play chess or to translate languages. Narrow AI systems are often called "expert systems" because they are designed to perform a task at a level of expertise comparable to a human expert.
- General AI: A type of AI designed to perform any task a human can. General AI is still in its early stages of development, and it is not yet clear if it will ever be possible to create a general AI system. However, if a general AI system were to be created, it would be able to learn and adapt to new situations, and it would

be able to perform a wide range of tasks, such as driving a car, writing a book, or diagnosing a disease.

- Superintelligent AI: A type of AI that is more intelligent than any human. Superintelligent AI is a theoretical concept, and it is unclear if creating a superintelligent AI system will ever be possible. If a superintelligent AI system were to be created, it would be able to solve problems that are currently beyond the capabilities of humans, and it could potentially pose a threat to humanity. The future of AI is uncertain. AI systems may eventually become so powerful that they will threaten humanity. However, it is also possible that AI systems will be used to solve some of the world's most pressing problems. Only time will tell what the future holds for AI.

Chapter 3: AI in Today's World - Applications and Implications

Artificial intelligence (AI) is no longer a distant concept confined to science fiction; it is a reality that permeates every aspect of our daily lives. As a result, AI has become an integral part of our everyday life, from the smartphones in our pockets to the smart homes we live in. In the business world, AI transforms industries from healthcare to finance, driving innovation and improving efficiency. In the next chapters, I will delve into the applications and implications of AI in various aspects of today's world.

AI in Everyday Life: From Smartphones to Smart Homes

Our smartphones are one of the most visible applications of AI in everyday life. Personal assistants like Apple's Siri, Google's Assistant, and Amazon's Alexa use AI to interpret our commands, answer our questions, and even learn our preferences over time. These systems use machine learning, AI, to learn and improve from experience. For example, they can learn to recognize our voices, understand our routines, and predict our needs.

Social media platforms like Facebook, TikTok, and Instagram use AI for personalized content delivery. They analyze our likes, shares, and interactions to understand our preferences and deliver content we are likely interested in. This not only improves user experience but also increases engagement.

Smart homes have also become a reality thanks to AI. Home automation systems use AI to control various aspects of our homes, including lighting, heating, and security. These systems can learn our routines and preferences to provide a customized living experience. For instance, a smart thermostat can automatically learn and adjust our preferred temperature settings. Likewise, a smart security system can recognize familiar faces and alert us when a stranger is detected.

AI in Business: From Healthcare to Finance and Beyond

In the business world, AI is revolutionizing various industries by enabling automation, improving decision-making, and providing insights from big data.

In healthcare, AI is used for various purposes, such as diagnosing diseases, predicting patient outcomes, and personalizing treatment plans. For example, AI algorithms can analyze medical images to detect abnormalities, such as tumors in MRI scans or signs of pneumonia in chest X-rays. AI can also analyze electronic health records to predict a patient's risk of developing certain diseases or complications, enabling early intervention.

In finance, AI is used for fraud detection, risk management, and algorithmic trading. For example, AI algorithms can detect unusual activity in a user's account, which could indicate fraud. They can also analyze market data to assess risk and make trading decisions. In addition, some robo-advisors use AI to provide personalized investment advice to clients.

Beyond healthcare and finance, AI is also transforming the retail, transportation, and manufacturing industries. In retail, AI is used for personalized marketing, inventory management, and demand forecasting. In transportation, AI powers self-driving cars and optimize logistics. Finally, AI is used for quality control, predictive maintenance, and production planning in manufacturing.

Real-World Examples of AI in Action

The applications of AI in everyday life and business are not just theoretical; they are real and tangible. Here are a few examples:

- Google's DeepMind developed an AI system called AlphaGo that defeated the world champion of Go, a game considered more complex than chess. This landmark achievement in AI demonstrated its ability to learn and strategize.

- IBM's Watson, an AI system, is used in healthcare to assist doctors in diagnosing diseases and recommending treatment options. For example, Watson can analyze a patient's medical history and a vast medical literature database to provide insights that a human doctor might miss.
- Amazon's recommendation system uses AI to suggest products to customers based on their browsing history, past purchases, and items in their cart. This system has been highly successful in increasing sales and improving customer experience.
- Tesla's Autopilot system uses AI to enable semi-autonomous driving. For example, the system can control the vehicle's speed, change lanes, and park the car. This is a prime example of how AI is being used to advance the field of autonomous vehicles.

Microsoft Copilot 2023

Microsoft Copilot is an AI software designed to help users with their productivity. It is a large language model (LLM) trained on a massive dataset of text and code. This allows Copilot to generate text, translate languages, write creative content, and answer your questions informally. Copilot is currently in preview and is available to Microsoft 365 subscribers. It is expected to be released to the general public in early 2023. Copilot can be used for a variety of tasks, including:

- Writing emails
- Creating presentations
- Writing code
- Translating languages
- Answering questions

- Generating creative content
- Cross-platform communication

Copilot is still under development as of May 2023 but can potentially revolutionize our work. It can help us be more productive, creative, and efficient.

Here are some examples of how Copilot can be used:

- You can use Copilot to write emails. Start typing your email, and Copilot will suggest text to help you complete your message.
- You can use Copilot to create presentations. Copilot can help you brainstorm ideas, write content, and design slides.
- You can use Copilot to write code. Copilot can help you to write code faster and more accurately.
- You can use Copilot to translate languages. Copilot can translate text from one language to another.
- You can use Copilot to answer questions. Copilot can answer your questions in a comprehensive and informative way.
- You can use Copilot to generate creative content. For example, Copilot can help you to write poems, stories, scripts, and more.
- Copilot is a powerful tool that can help you to be more productive and creative. It is still under development, but it can potentially revolutionize our work.

The Implications of AI

While AI has many benefits, it also has implications that must be carefully considered. These include issues related to privacy, job displacement, and ethical considerations.

Privacy is a major concern with AI, as many AI systems rely on personal data. This raises questions about how this data is collected, used, and protected. Therefore, it is crucial for companies to have clear data privacy policies and for users to be aware of how their data is being used. AI also can potentially displace jobs, especially those involving repetitive tasks. While AI can create new jobs by opening up new fields and opportunities, the transition can be challenging for those whose jobs are displaced.

Ethically, AI also poses several challenges. For instance, using AI in decision-making could lead to bias if the data used to train the AI system is biased. Furthermore, using AI in areas like autonomous weapons raises serious ethical and safety concerns. AI is a powerful technology transforming our everyday life and business. While it brings many benefits, it has significant implications that must be carefully managed. As we continue to embrace AI, it is crucial to foster a culture of responsible AI use, ensuring that it is used to benefit society as a whole.

Chapter 4: The Ethical and Societal Implications of AI

Artificial Intelligence (AI) has undeniably revolutionized our world, embedding itself in every facet of our lives, from personal devices to business models. However, while AI is a powerful tool with vast potential, it raises complex ethical and societal implications simultaneously. These implications range from the realm of governance, including surveillance and crime prevention, to broader social and economic implications that affect individuals, communities, and societies.

AI in Governance: Surveillance, Crime Prevention, and Public Services

AI has become a potent tool in governance, with applications in surveillance, crime prevention, and the provision of public services. The advent of AI has transformed surveillance. AI-powered facial recognition technology, for instance, is employed in public spaces to identify individuals in real-time. This has been touted as a powerful tool for maintaining security and order. However, it raises serious ethical concerns. These include concerns about privacy, the potential for misuse, and the risk of false positives leading to unjust consequences. Additionally, there are concerns about bias, as facial recognition algorithms are less accurate for people of color and women.

In crime prevention, AI systems predict potential criminal activity and allocate police resources accordingly. These predictive policing systems analyze data on past crimes to identify patterns and predict future crime hotspots. While these systems can enhance efficiency and effectiveness, they raise significant ethical questions. For example, if the data used to train the system is biased, the system's predictions may reinforce and exacerbate existing biases and inequalities in the criminal justice system.

AI also has applications in public services. For example, AI-powered chatbots are used to streamline citizen interactions with government agencies, and AI algorithms are used to optimize the allocation of public resources. However, these applications also have ethical implications. For example, there are concerns about transparency, accountability, and the risk of bias in decision-making.

The Social and Economic Implications of AI

AI's impact extends far beyond governance, with profound social and economic implications. On the social front, AI has the potential to both bridge and widen divides. AI can democratize access to information and services, reduce barriers for people with disabilities, and enhance social connectivity. However, it can also exacerbate social inequalities. For example, those with access to AI technology may gain advantages in education and job opportunities, leaving those without access behind. There are also concerns about the impact of AI on social interactions and mental health.

Economically, AI can drive growth, innovation, and efficiency. It can potentially create new industries, transform existing ones, and enhance productivity. However, AI also poses significant economic challenges. Job displacement is a major concern, as AI has the potential to automate a wide range of tasks, from manufacturing to customer service. While AI can also create new jobs, the transition can be challenging, particularly for those lacking the skills needed for the new jobs.

Furthermore, AI has implications for economic inequality. The economic benefits of AI are likely to be unevenly distributed, with those owning and controlling AI technology standing to gain the most. This raises concerns about the concentration of wealth and power.

While AI offers immense potential, it also raises complex ethical and societal implications that must be carefully considered and managed. This requires a multi-faceted approach involving ethical guidelines for AI development and use, legal and regulatory frameworks, education and awareness-raising, and ongoing research and dialogue. Moreover, as AI continues to evolve and permeate our society, ensuring that it serves the common good and does not exacerbate existing inequalities is crucial.

Chapter 5: AI Ethics - The Debate on AI and Humanity

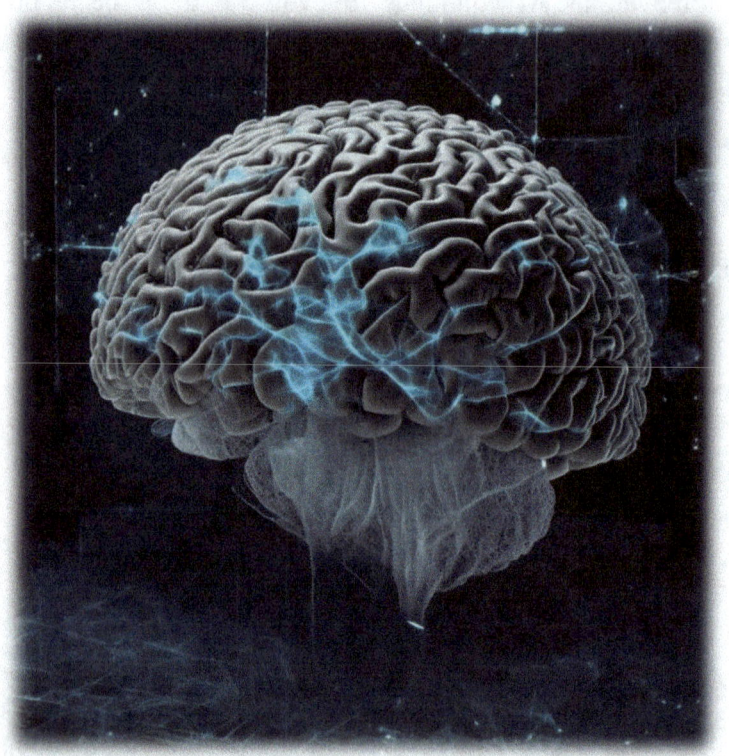

As artificial intelligence (AI) continues to evolve and permeate various aspects of our lives, it has sparked critical debates on its ethical implications and its relationship with humanity. These debates encompass a wide array of issues, including AI's moral and ethical considerations, the question of AI rights and responsibilities, issues of AI bias and fairness, and the role of regulation in AI development.

The Moral and Ethical Considerations of AI

AI, by its nature, poses numerous moral and ethical challenges. The deployment of AI impacts decision-making processes, privacy, security, and even the nature of human work. AI systems are often designed to make decisions based on data. This could range from trivial decisions like recommending a movie to a user to life-altering ones like approving a loan application or diagnosing a disease. An ethical dilemma arises when these AI systems make mistakes, or their decision-making process is opaque, often called the 'black box' problem. This lack of transparency can lead to a lack of accountability, making it difficult to ascertain blame when things go wrong.

Privacy and security are also significant ethical issues. AI systems, particularly those used in surveillance or data analysis, often have access to sensitive personal data. This data could infringe on individual privacy rights or lead to identity theft or fraud if misused. Hence, the development and use of AI must be conducted to respect privacy and ensure data security.

AI also raises ethical considerations about the future of work. With AI's potential to automate many jobs, there are concerns about job displacement and the need for humans to re-skill or up-skill.

The Debate over AI Rights and Responsibilities

As AI systems become more sophisticated, there is a growing debate over whether they should have rights and responsibilities. This discussion is particularly relevant to autonomous systems that can learn, adapt, and make decisions without human intervention. The question of AI rights is controversial. On the one hand, some argue that if an AI system can demonstrate human-like consciousness or sentience, it might be entitled to certain rights. On the other hand, others argue that rights are intrinsically tied to human experiences and biology and, thus, should not be extended to AI.

The question of AI responsibilities is equally complex. Who is responsible if an autonomous AI system makes a decision that leads to harm? Is it the system itself, the developers who created it, the users who deployed it, or the legislators who allowed its use? Addressing this issue is vital for accountability and justice.

AI Bias and Fairness

AI systems learn from data, and if this data is biased, the AI system can also become biased, leading to unfair outcomes. Bias in AI can manifest in various ways, such as racial or gender bias in facial recognition technology, loan approval systems, or hiring algorithms. This has serious implications for fairness and equality.

The issue of AI bias and fairness is not just a technical problem but a social one. Therefore, it requires technical solutions like better algorithms, more diverse training data, and societal solutions like bias awareness and inclusive practices in AI development.

The Role of Regulation in AI Development

Regulation plays a crucial role in guiding the development and use of AI. Regulations can set AI transparency, accountability, privacy, and fairness standards. They can also address issues such as AI rights and responsibilities, AI bias, and the social and economic implications of AI. However, regulating AI is a complex task. It requires a balance between fostering innovation and preventing harm. It also requires international cooperation, as AI technology is global. Regulations must be adaptable to keep up with the rapid pace of AI development. They also need to be inclusive and consider the diverse perspectives of stakeholders, including AI developers, users, and those affected by AI.

Finally, the ethics of AI is a multi-faceted and complex field that prompts critical discussions on various issues. As we continue to integrate AI into our lives, it is essential that we continually assess and address these ethical considerations. From ensuring fairness, eliminating bias, defining rights and responsibilities, and establishing effective regulations, each step should be grounded in promoting the common good and preserving human dignity. As we navigate the AI ethics landscape, we must remember that technology should always serve humanity, not vice versa.

Chapter 6: The Future of AI - Possibilities, Predictions, and Preparations

Artificial Intelligence (AI) has grown extraordinarily in the last few decades, impacting almost every sector of society and economy. As we look forward to the future of AI, it is essential to consider the possibilities, predictions, and necessary preparations to harness this technology responsibly and beneficially.

Future Applications of AI: From Climate Change to Space Exploration

AI's potential for future applications is vast and diverse, with the power to address some of the most pressing challenges of our time. In addressing climate change, AI can play a pivotal role. It can optimize energy use in buildings, vehicles, and factories, reducing greenhouse gas emissions. AI can also help in climate modeling, making predictions more accurate and thus improving our understanding of the impact of climate change. It can be used in environmental monitoring, aiding in detecting and preventing deforestation, illegal fishing, and other harmful activities. In the realm of space exploration, AI can assist in various ways. For example, it can help analyze vast amounts of data collected by telescopes to detect new celestial bodies or phenomena. AI can also be used in autonomous spacecraft navigation and the operation of robotic exploration vehicles on other planets.

Predictions for the Future of AI: The Optimists and the Pessimists

Predictions of AI often fall into two camps: the optimists and the pessimists. The optimists see a future where AI will continue to drive economic growth, improve our quality of life, and help solve pressing global issues like climate change, poverty, and disease. Moreover, they believe that the benefits of AI will outweigh the potential risks and that humanity will find ways to manage these risks.

On the other hand, the pessimists caution about the potential negative impacts of AI. They worry about job displacement due to automation, the misuse of AI for malicious purposes, and the possibility of a superintelligent AI that could pose an existential threat to humanity. Therefore, they argue for AI's careful and responsible development, with robust safeguards and regulations.

The Societal Impact of Advanced AI: Job Displacement and New Opportunities

As AI continues to advance, it will undoubtedly have significant societal impacts. One of the most discussed is job displacement due to automation. Many jobs, particularly those involving routine or repetitive tasks, are at risk of being automated by AI. This includes jobs in manufacturing, transportation, and even some areas of customer service and administration.

However, while AI may displace some jobs, it also has the potential to create new ones. These new jobs could arise in AI development and management, in sectors transformed by AI, and in new industries that AI could create. Furthermore, AI can increase productivity, leading to economic growth and new opportunities.

Preparing for an AI-driven Future: Education and Policy Recommendations

Investing in education and policy is essential to prepare for an AI-driven future. Regarding education, it is crucial to equip people with the skills to thrive in an AI-driven world. This includes technical skills like programming and data analysis and skills like critical thinking, creativity, and emotional intelligence that AI is unlikely to replicate. In addition, lifelong learning and re-skilling should be encouraged to help people adapt as the job market changes due to AI.

Policy-wise, governments need to create robust legal and regulatory frameworks to guide the development and use of AI. These frameworks should promote AI transparency, accountability, and fairness, protect privacy and security, and address issues like job displacement and economic inequality. In addition, they should be flexible enough to adapt to the rapid pace of AI development yet robust enough to prevent misuse and mitigate risks. The future of AI holds great promise but also significant challenges. As we navigate this future, it is crucial to consider the potential applications of AI, understand the diverse predictions, acknowledge the societal impacts, and prepare through education and policy measures. By doing so, we can harness the power of AI to benefit society while mitigating potential risks. The journey toward an AI-driven future requires careful navigation, collective effort, and a strong commitment to upholding ethical standards and promoting the common good.

Chapter 7: AI and Data - The Fuel of the Future

Artificial intelligence (AI) and data are intrinsically linked, with data as the critical fuel powering AI systems. This relationship between AI and data has profound implications for developing and using AI and managing and protecting data. This discussion delves into the role of data in AI, the implications of big data for AI development, and the importance of data privacy and security in AI.

Understanding the Role of Data in AI

Data is at the heart of AI. AI systems, particularly those using machine learning techniques, learn from data to make predictions or decisions without being explicitly programmed to perform the task. For instance, a machine learning model trained to identify spam would be fed many emails labeled 'spam' or 'not spam.' The model would learn from these examples to identify patterns or characteristics that distinguish spam emails from non-spam ones. Once trained, the model can analyze new, unlabeled emails and predict whether they are spam. In this way, data serves as both the teacher and the test for AI systems: it provides the examples from which the system learns and the cases on which it is tested and evaluated. The quality, diversity, and quantity of this data are critical to the effectiveness of the AI system.

Big Data and Its Implications for AI Development

The advent of big data – massive volumes of data generated from various sources at high velocity – has significant implications for AI development.

Firstly, big data provides a rich source of information for training AI systems. The more data an AI system has to learn from, the better it can become at its task. Big data can help AI systems uncover complex patterns and relationships that would be impossible to detect with smaller datasets.

Secondly, big data can enable the development of more sophisticated AI systems. With large amounts of data, AI systems can tackle complex problems that require deep learning, a subset of machine learning that uses neural networks with many layers to model high-level abstractions in data.

However, the use of big data in AI also presents challenges. One is the risk of overfitting, where an AI system becomes too tuned to the training data and performs poorly on new, unseen data. Another challenge is ensuring the quality and representativeness of the data, as biases in the data can lead to biases in the AI system's predictions or decisions.

The Importance of Data Privacy and Security in AI

Data privacy and security are paramount because AI systems often rely on personal or sensitive data. Data privacy concerns the rights of individuals over their data. When personal data is used to train or operate an AI system, it is essential to ensure that the individual's privacy rights are respected. This includes obtaining informed consent for data use, ensuring data is used only for the purposes for which consent was given, and anonymizing data to protect individuals' identities.

Data security, on the other hand, involves protecting data from unauthorized access or loss. Therefore, AI developers and operators must implement robust security measures to prevent data breaches, which could lead to data misuse and harm to individuals. Moreover, as AI systems become more prevalent and data-driven, there is a growing need for transparency and accountability in how data is used in AI. This involves explaining how data is used to train AI systems, how these systems make decisions based on data, and who is responsible when these decisions lead to harmful outcomes.

In conclusion, data is indeed the fuel of AI, powering its development and operation. As we continue to harness the power of AI, it is essential to understand the role of data in AI, the implications of big data, and the importance of data privacy and security. By doing so, we can ensure that our use of AI is effective but also ethical, responsible, and respectful of individual rights. This careful stewardship of data is crucial as we navigate the future of AI, a future that promises immense potential but also demands our vigilance and responsibility.

Chapter 8: The Role of AI in Cybersecurity

Artificial intelligence (AI) is playing an increasingly significant role in cybersecurity. However, it is a double-edged sword, with capabilities that can be harnessed for both cyber defense and cyber offense. This discussion delves into the role of AI in cyber defense, including anomaly detection, threat prediction, and response, and the rising concern about AI-powered cyber-attacks.

AI in Cyber Defense: Anomaly Detection, Threat Prediction, and Response

AI's ability to process vast amounts of data and identify patterns makes it a valuable tool in cyber defense. There are three key areas where AI is particularly useful: anomaly detection, threat prediction, and response.

- Anomaly Detection: AI can monitor network traffic and user behavior, learning what 'normal' patterns look like. Once it has a baseline, it can detect anomalies – patterns that deviate from the norm. These anomalies can indicate cyber threats like malware infections or data breaches. AI's ability to detect anomalies in real-time allows for swift detection of potential threats, which is crucial in minimizing damage.
- Threat Prediction: AI can also predict threats before they occur. AI systems can identify patterns and trends that signal an impending attack by analyzing historical cyber-attack data and keeping current with the latest threat intelligence. This predictive capability allows organizations to strengthen their defenses and prevent attacks proactively.
- Response: Quickly responding is critical to minimize damage during a cyber-attack. AI can aid in this by automating certain response processes. For example, if an AI system detects a malware infection, it could automatically isolate the infected device from the network to prevent it from spreading. AI can also assist in incident response by helping identify the source and nature of the attack, aiding recovery efforts.

AI in Cyber Offense: The Rise of AI-Powered Cyber Attacks

While AI can be a powerful tool for cyber defense, it can also be used for cyber offense. Cybercriminals are increasingly leveraging AI to conduct more sophisticated and damaging attacks. In addition, AI can automate cyber-attacks, allowing attackers to launch attacks at scale and speed that would be impossible for humans. For instance, AI can automate the process of scanning for vulnerabilities in a network and exploiting them.

AI can also be used to create more convincing phishing attacks. By analyzing data on a target, an AI system could craft personalized phishing emails that are more likely to trick the target into clicking a malicious link or providing sensitive information.

Furthermore, AI can create 'deep fakes' – manipulated audio or video content that is incredibly convincing. These deepfakes can be used for misinformation campaigns, identity theft, or to trick individuals or systems into revealing sensitive information. The role of AI in cybersecurity is significant and multi-faceted. It offers powerful tools for defense, enhancing our ability to detect, predict, and respond to cyber threats. However, using AI in cyber offenses presents new challenges that require ongoing research, vigilance, and the development of advanced defensive strategies. As we continue to harness the power of AI in cybersecurity, it is crucial to remain mindful of these dual aspects and strive to use AI responsibly and ethically in the cybersecurity realm.

Chapter 9: AI and Healthcare - Saving Lives with Algorithms

Integrating artificial intelligence (AI) into healthcare has transformative potential, enhancing diagnostics, treatment, and patient care and paving the way for a future of personalized medicine and advanced healthcare applications. However, these advancements also bring ethical considerations that must be carefully addressed. This discussion explores the role of AI in healthcare, the future of AI in this sector, and the ethical implications.

AI in Diagnostics, Treatment, and Patient Care

AI holds significant promise in enhancing various aspects of healthcare, including diagnostics, treatment, and patient care.

- Diagnostics: AI algorithms, particularly those using machine learning, can analyze medical images (like CT scans, MRIs, and X-rays) or genetic data to detect diseases. For instance, AI has been used to develop models that can identify cancerous tumors in medical images with a level of accuracy comparable to, or in some cases even surpassing, that of trained human specialists.
- Treatment: AI is also being integrated into the treatment process. Predictive analytics, powered by AI, can assist healthcare providers in determining the most effective treatment plans for patients, considering various variables such as medical history, genetic factors, and lifestyle. AI can also assist in drug discovery, accelerating the identification and development of new therapeutic compounds.
- Patient Care: In inpatient care, AI can monitor patient health and recommend personalized care. AI-powered wearable devices can track various health metrics, alerting patients and healthcare providers to potential health concerns before they become serious. In addition, AI chatbots can provide patients with instant access to medical advice and information, enhancing patient engagement and education.

The Future of AI in Healthcare: Personalized Medicine, AI Surgeons, and More

The future of AI in healthcare extends beyond diagnostics, treatment, and patient care to potentially revolutionary applications.

- Personalized Medicine: With the ability to analyze vast amounts of data, AI can enable a more personalized approach to medicine. By considering an individual's genetic makeup, lifestyle, and environmental factors, AI systems can predict more accurately how an individual will respond to a certain treatment or risk of developing specific diseases. This could lead to customized treatment plans that optimize efficacy and minimize side effects.
- AI Surgeons: There is ongoing research into the use of AI in surgery, with robotic surgery systems being an active development area. These systems could potentially perform certain surgical procedures with high precision and consistency.

Despite the promise, it is important to note that integrating AI into such critical tasks will require rigorous testing, validation, and regulatory oversight to ensure safety and efficacy.

Ethical Considerations in AI Healthcare

As AI becomes more integrated into healthcare, several ethical considerations arise.

- Patient Privacy: AI systems must often access sensitive patient data to function effectively. Ensuring this data is used responsibly and safeguarded effectively is crucial to maintaining patient trust and complying with data protection regulations.

- Bias: If the data used to train AI systems is biased, the systems may make biased predictions. This could lead to certain groups receiving lower-quality care, a significant ethical concern.

- Transparency and Accountability: As AI systems become more involved in patient care, questions arise about who is responsible when things go wrong. Is it the doctors using the AI system, the developers who created it, or the AI system itself? Transparency in how AI systems make decisions is important to ensure trust and accountability.

AI has tremendous potential to revolutionize healthcare, improving diagnostics, treatment, and patient care and opening new frontiers like personalized medicine and AI-assisted surgery. However, as we embrace the benefits of AI in healthcare, it is crucial to address the ethical considerations that arise. Patient privacy, bias, transparency, and accountability are key issues that must be carefully managed to ensure that the use of AI in healthcare is responsible, fair, and in patients' best interests. Furthermore, as we navigate this exciting future, it is essential to ensure that AI is used to enhance healthcare while upholding the highest ethical standards. This balanced approach will allow us to harness the full potential of AI in healthcare, ultimately driving better outcomes for patients and the healthcare system as a whole.

Chapter 10: AI and the Environment - A Double-Edged Sword

Artificial intelligence (AI) has a complex relationship with the environment, both as a powerful tool for promoting sustainability and posing environmental challenges. This discussion explores the role of AI in combating climate change, the environmental footprint of AI, and the prospects for green AI.

The Role of AI in Combating Climate Change and Promoting Sustainability

AI can serve as a valuable ally in the fight against climate change and the pursuit of sustainability, with applications spanning various sectors.

- Climate Modeling and Prediction: AI can enhance our ability to model climate systems and predict climate change impacts. Machine learning algorithms can analyze vast amounts of climate data, identifying patterns and trends that can inform climate change mitigation and adaptation strategies.
- Energy Efficiency: AI can optimize energy use in multiple settings. AI can manage energy consumption in homes and buildings by controlling heating, cooling, and lighting systems based on occupancy and usage patterns. On a larger scale, AI can optimize the operation of power grids, balancing supply and demand more efficiently and integrating renewable energy sources effectively.
- Sustainable Agriculture: AI can help make agriculture more sustainable. Machine learning models can predict crop yields, optimize irrigation, and detect pests or diseases, reducing the use of water and chemicals and improving food security.
- Conservation: AI can also aid in wildlife conservation. AI algorithms can analyze drone images or camera traps to monitor wildlife populations, track animal movements, and detect poaching activities.

The Environmental Footprint of AI: Energy Use and

E-Waste

While AI can help promote sustainability, it also has an environmental footprint that must be considered.

- Energy Use: Training AI models, particularly large deep learning models, requires substantial computational power and energy. The energy use associated with AI has grown as models become more complex and datasets larger.
- E-Waste: The hardware used to run AI models can contribute to electronic waste (e-waste) once it reaches the end of its lifespan. E-waste is a growing environmental problem due to the hazardous materials it contains and the challenges associated with recycling it.

Future Prospects for Green AI

The dual environmental implications of AI have led to growing interest in 'green AI,' an approach that aims to harness the environmental benefits of AI while minimizing its environmental footprint.

One avenue for green AI is the development of more energy-efficient AI algorithms and hardware. Researchers are exploring reducing the computational resources needed to train AI models without compromising performance. This includes techniques like model pruning (removing unnecessary parts of the model), knowledge distillation (training a smaller model to mimic a larger one), and more efficient hardware.

There is also a need for greater transparency about the environmental impact of AI. For instance, this could involve reporting the carbon emissions of training an AI model. Moreover, the principles of circular economy can be applied to manage the e-waste associated with AI hardware. This involves designing for longevity, repairability, and recyclability, promoting reuse and recycling, and incorporating recycled materials into new products. AI presents both opportunities and challenges for the environment. It can be a powerful tool in combating climate change and promoting sustainability, but its environmental footprint cannot be ignored. Therefore, as we continue to develop and use AI, it is crucial to strive for a green AI approach that maximizes the environmental benefits of AI while minimizing its environmental impact. This balanced approach will allow us to harness the power of AI in a way that is not only technologically advanced and effective but also environmentally responsible and sustainable.

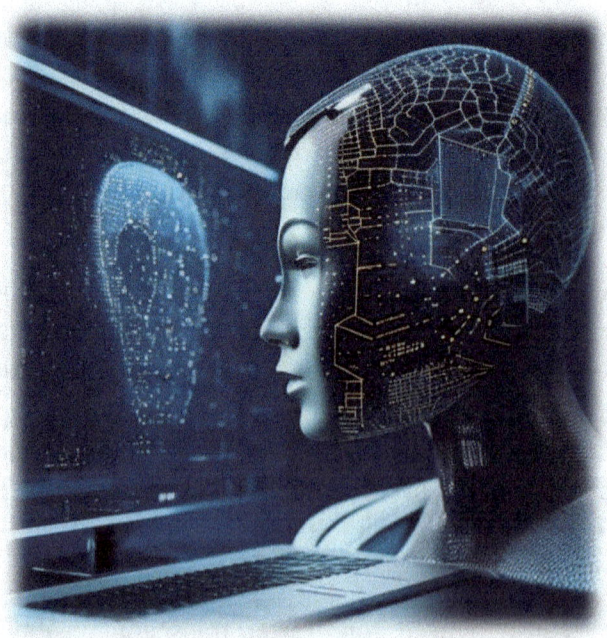

Chapter 11: AI and Entertainment - The Changing Face of Media

Artificial Intelligence has permeated every aspect of our lives, and the realm of entertainment is no exception. As a technology that has the potential to learn and mimic human behaviors, AI is reshaping the landscape of entertainment, transforming the way we interact with video games, movies, music, and even social media influencers.

AI in Video Games, Movies, and Music

Video Games: AI has been an integral part of video games for decades, often used to control non-player characters (NPCs) and to create dynamic, responsive game environments. However, AI technology has advanced significantly in recent years, and these advances are used to create more sophisticated and immersive gaming experiences. For example, machine learning algorithms are now used to improve NPC behavior, making them more unpredictable and realistic. In addition, procedural content generation, powered by AI, is also being used to create vast, complex game worlds that can adapt to a player's actions.

AI is used in various ways in the film industry, from scriptwriting to post-production. AI algorithms are used to analyze scripts, predict viewer responses, and generate scenes or full movies. For example, the short film "Sunspring" was entirely written by an AI, using predictive text based on a database of science fiction screenplays. In post-production, AI is used for tasks like color grading and special effects, significantly reducing the time and cost of these processes.

AI's impact on music has been profound, from composition to production and distribution. AI algorithms can now generate original compositions in various styles and moods. Artists and producers use AI tools to aid in songwriting, creating new melodies and lyrics. AI is also used in music mastering, traditionally done by sound engineers. Platforms like LANDR use AI to analyze and process music tracks, providing a quicker and more accessible mastering solution.

The Rise of AI Influencers and Digital Artists

AI is also making its way into social media and digital art, giving rise to AI influencers and artists. These AI personas, like Lil Miquela, are entirely digital creations that interact with real people on social media platforms, sharing their 'lives,' endorsing products, and even engaging in social issues. While not real, these influencers have amassed significant followings, blurring the lines between reality and the digital world.

In digital art, AI is being used to create new works and styles. Artists often use AI algorithms to generate art with stunning and unique results. AI has also been used to create new works in the style of deceased artists, raising interesting questions about authorship and creativity.

The Future of Entertainment in an AI-driven World

The future of entertainment in an AI-driven world is exciting and full of potential. As AI technology advances, we can expect even more immersive and personalized entertainment experiences. We can anticipate even more intelligent NPCs and dynamically evolving game worlds in gaming. We may also see the rise of fully AI-driven games, where the story and world adapt to the player's actions in real-time.

AI could be used in film and television to create fully digital actors, reducing the need for costly CGI and stunt doubles. AI could also adapt content to the viewer, changing plotlines and endings based on viewer preferences.

In music, AI could democratize music production, making it easier for anyone to compose, produce, and master their music. We may also see more collaboration between human artists and AI, creating new genres and styles of music.

The rise of AI influencers and digital artists will likely continue and become more interactive. AI in the media and entertainment sector, currently worth $13 billion with a compound annual growth rate of 26%, is set to be worth a staggering $99.3 billion by 2030. The need for production companies, studios, streaming platforms, broadcasters, distributors, and exhibitors to understand their audiences better drives this immense growth. AI and machine learning will change the guessing game that the media and entertainment industry has grown accustomed to, often with hundreds of millions of dollars on line. As said by Mayer, a prominent figure in the entertainment industry, the future of entertainment will be significantly influenced by AI. Streaming platforms already use data, not for the creative per se, but to identify audience preferences, including the kind of programming they love, the stars they prefer, and the most engaging formats and timing. Social media platforms have also capitalized on AI and machine learning to personalize user experiences and create massive traction, even with low-budget unprofessional content.

For instance, a platform like TikTok uses AI to understand an individual's preferences and deliver exactly what they are interested in. This AI-driven personalization is part of the future of the entertainment industry, as it brings low-production value content to life and engages people massively. From a tech perspective, machine learning and AI are the future. As Malik Kurdi, the founder of Exemplary Marketing, noted, understanding audiences and learning about them more efficiently is a massive barrier to growth. AI and machine learning can help to overcome this barrier by making life easier for viewers and app users. With these technologies, corporations can make more accurate decisions and investments, and app developers can create apps that constantly evolve with the consumer experience.

The future of entertainment in an AI-driven world will likely be much more personalized and immersive. As the demand for technology in this area is skyrocketing, the scope and usage of AI are set to become much more ingrained in society for commercial growth and consumer efficiency. This evolution promises exciting times ahead for creators and consumers alike, with AI leading the way in transforming how we engage with entertainment.

Chapter 12: AI and the Job Market - Opportunities and Threats

Artificial Intelligence (AI) is another technological development revolutionizing how we work, communicate, and interact with the world. This revolution brings both opportunities and threats, particularly regarding the job market. Therefore, AI's impact on job displacement and creation, the changing nature of work, and the preparations needed for an AI-driven world are all critical considerations.

The Impact of AI on Job Displacement and Creation

- Job Displacement: AI has the potential to automate numerous tasks, which has significant implications for the job market. Jobs that involve repetitive tasks, data analysis, and even some elements of customer service are at risk of being automated. This displacement is particularly pronounced in the manufacturing, transport, and service industries.

- Job Creation: On the flip side, AI is also a significant job creator. As a new technology, specialists must develop, maintain, and improve AI systems. This need creates new roles in AI development, data science, and AI ethics. Furthermore, as businesses incorporate AI into their operations, they will require staff who understand AI and can work alongside it. Therefore, new roles not present before AI's advent are being created.

The Changing Nature of Work in an AI-Driven World

As AI becomes more integrated into workplaces, the nature of work is changing. Jobs will likely become more focused on tasks that AI cannot or cannot do well. These include creative tasks, strategic decision-making, and jobs that require a high level of emotional intelligence. Furthermore, as AI takes over more mundane and repetitive tasks, employees could focus on more meaningful and engaging aspects of their jobs. This shift could lead to increased job satisfaction and efficiency.

However, this also means that employees must continually adapt to new technology and possibly retrain for new roles. This continual change can create uncertainty and stress for workers who must keep up with the ever-evolving workplace.

Preparing the Workforce for AI: Education and Training

Preparing the workforce for an AI-driven world requires both education and training. First, we must educate the next generation of workers about AI and its implications. This education should start at school, with children learning about AI and other advanced technologies. Furthermore, there needs to be an emphasis on lifelong learning. As AI evolves, workers will need to update their skills continuously. This need for constant learning will require a shift in how we view education and training, with a greater focus on continuous professional development and retraining.

In conclusion, AI presents both opportunities and threats to the job market. While it may displace some jobs, it also creates new ones. The nature of work is changing, shifting towards tasks that AI cannot do well. Preparing for this future requires focusing on education and training to ensure that workers can adapt to the AI-driven world.

Chapter 13: AI Governance – The Need for Oversight and Regulation

AI governance and regulation is a rapidly evolving field driven by the increasing influence of AI technologies on various aspects of society. Furthermore, as AI systems become more integrated into various sectors, such as media and entertainment, there is a growing need for comprehensive and adaptable regulatory frameworks to oversee their use and mitigate potential risks.

The Current State of AI Governance and Regulation

As of 2023, AI governance is recognized as one of the main challenges facing privacy professionals, with data governance becoming increasingly complex due to the capacity of AI and machine learning technologies to collect and process large volumes of data rapidly. As a result, there is a growing recognition of the need for AI governance, with privacy professionals often being some of the first individuals called upon when organizations begin considering how to approach this issue.

Challenges and Considerations in Creating AI Policy

There are numerous challenges associated with creating an AI policy. These include understanding how to manage and protect data effectively, addressing biases in automated decision-making tools, preventing the misuse of personal information, and regulating the collection and management of personal information by AI systems. In addition, as AI technologies evolve, regulatory frameworks must be continually updated to keep pace with changes and advancements in the field.

Organizations are often challenged with understanding their obligations in different jurisdictions, which is particularly relevant for multinational organizations that must navigate many national and regional laws and regulations. Additionally, there is a pressing need for more privacy professionals with a comprehensive understanding of data, technology, risk management, user design, business processes, and product and technology design.

Case Studies of AI Governance Around the World

AI governance is being addressed at both national and international levels. For example, in the United States, multiple states, including Alabama, Colorado, Mississippi, Vermont, and Washington, are reviewing and enacting regulations governing how AI can collect and manage personal information. At the federal level, the Federal Trade Commission (FTC) is investigating potential new rules for using AI by commercial organizations, specifically focusing on inaccuracy, bias, discrimination, and commercial surveillance issues. Furthermore, the National Institute of Standards and Technology (NIST) is developing an AI Risk Management Framework (AI RMF) to manage better the risks associated with AI to individuals, organizations, and society.

In the European Union, the European Commission has proposed the Artificial Intelligence Act (AI Act), a set of harmonized rules on artificial intelligence, which is expected to be voted on by the European Parliament in March 2023 and could begin enforcement in 2026.

Despite this overview, areas still require further exploration to provide a complete picture of the state of AI governance and regulation. For example, more recent developments or case studies from other world regions are essential to understand the global impact of AI. Also, a more detailed analysis of the challenges and considerations in creating AI policy could include exploring ethical considerations, the role of public perception and understanding of AI, and the balance between innovation and regulation.

Chapter 14: AI and Global Politics - The New Arms Race

Artificial Intelligence (AI) has rapidly evolved in recent years, leading to advancements that were once only imaginable in science fiction. These developments have significant implications for global politics, with AI becoming a new frontier in the international arms race. As a result, AI has begun to reshape military and defense strategies, influence power dynamics on a global scale, and raise critical ethical questions surrounding autonomous weapons.

The Role of AI in Military and Defense

AI has a growing role in the military and defense sectors worldwide, providing new capabilities and transforming traditional approaches to warfare. A key application area is in intelligence, surveillance, and reconnaissance (ISR) operations. For example, advanced AI algorithms can sift through vast amounts of data gathered by satellites, drones, and other surveillance systems, identifying patterns and anomalies that human analysts might miss. This can significantly enhance threat detection, assessment accuracy, and speed, enabling more proactive and informed decision-making. AI is also being integrated into autonomous systems, such as uncrewed aerial vehicles (UAVs) and crewless ground vehicles (UGVs), which can carry out missions in environments that may be too dangerous for human soldiers. These systems can execute surveillance, reconnaissance, and even combat operations, reducing the risk to human life.

Moreover, AI has potential applications in logistics and maintenance in the military. For example, predictive maintenance algorithms can anticipate equipment failures before they occur, reducing downtime and extending the lifespan of critical assets. Similarly, AI can optimize logistics and supply chain operations, ensuring the efficient movement of personnel, equipment, and supplies.

However, the integration of AI into military operations is not without risks. The reliance on AI systems could lead to new vulnerabilities, such as susceptibility to adversarial AI attacks, where an opponent manipulates an AI system's input data to cause it to malfunction. There is also concern about the risk of accidents with autonomous systems, which could result in unintended civilian casualties or escalate conflicts.

AI as a Factor in Global Power Dynamics

Adopting AI technology is not just a matter of military strategy but also a factor influencing global power dynamics. Nations leading in AI research and development, such as the United States and China, stand to gain significant geopolitical advantages. Mastery of AI technology can offer economic, military, and intelligence advantages, solidifying a country's position on the world stage.

In the economic realm, AI can drive growth and productivity, giving nations an edge in global competition. Countries that can successfully apply AI in various sectors of their economies, from manufacturing to services, will likely experience increased economic prosperity. Military superiority, traditionally measured in physical assets and workforce, is also being redefined. A new form of digital arms race is taking shape, where supremacy in AI and other emerging technologies like quantum computing and cybersecurity is increasingly important. Advanced AI capabilities, from autonomous weapons systems to cyber warfare tools, can significantly boost a state's military strength. AI also has profound implications for global intelligence operations. The ability to process vast amounts of data quickly and accurately can give nations an advantage in gathering and analyzing intelligence. This could lead to significant shifts in geopolitical strategies and alliances.

The Ethics and Implications of Autonomous Weapons

The rise of AI in defense has triggered serious ethical debates, particularly regarding autonomous weapons systems. These systems, sometimes called "killer robots," can independently select and engage targets without human intervention. While these weapons could save lives by removing soldiers from harm's way, they also raise ethical and legal concerns. One of the most pressing concerns is the question of accountability. Determining who is to be held responsible is complex in an unlawful act or an act of war committed by an autonomous weapon. For example, who is responsible for unlawful acts: the developers who designed the AI, the military personnel who deployed it, or the policymakers who authorized its use?

AI and Global Politics - The New Arms Race

Artificial Intelligence (AI) is rapidly transforming global politics and has begun to influence the balance of power on the global stage. This paradigm shift is often called the "New Arms Race."

The Role of AI in Military and Defense

AI is increasingly adopted in military and defense applications because it can improve decision-making, enhance operational efficiency, and provide strategic advantages. AI can be used in intelligence analysis, threat identification, logistics, and autonomous systems.

AI's role in intelligence analysis involves processing large volumes of data to identify potential threats or areas of interest. This allows for more accurate and timely information, which can be critical in strategic decision-making. Furthermore, AI can be used in logistics to optimize the supply chain, manage resources, and predict maintenance needs, thereby reducing costs and improving readiness. A key area of interest in military AI applications is autonomous systems. These range from crewless vehicles (air, land, and sea) to autonomous weapons systems. Autonomous systems can operate in environments that are too dangerous or inaccessible for humans, and they can potentially perform tasks more efficiently and effectively than human-operated systems.

However, integrating AI into the military and defense is not without challenges. There are technical hurdles to overcome, such as ensuring the reliability and robustness of AI systems in the face of adversarial attacks. Additionally, using AI raises significant ethical and legal concerns, particularly regarding autonomous weapons systems.

AI as a Factor in Global Power Dynamics

AI is becoming a significant factor in global power dynamics. Countries that lead in AI technology can gain substantial economic, political, and military advantages.

From an economic perspective, AI can drive productivity and growth, and it is becoming a key factor in industries ranging from healthcare to finance to entertainment. As a result, countries that can harness the power of AI can potentially gain a competitive edge in the global economy.

Politically, AI can be used to influence public opinion, both domestically and internationally. This can be seen in the use of AI in information operations and cyber warfare. Additionally, countries with advanced AI capabilities may have greater influence in setting international norms and regulations around the use of AI.

From a military perspective, AI can provide strategic advantages, as discussed in the previous section. This has led to an "AI arms race," with countries worldwide investing heavily in AI research and development for military applications. This race is about developing more advanced AI technologies, attracting and retaining AI talent, and establishing the infrastructure to support AI development and deployment. One of the primary ethical concerns is the question of accountability. If an autonomous weapon causes unintended harm, who is responsible? Is it the developers who created the AI, the military personnel who deployed it, or the policymakers who approved its use?

There are also concerns about the potential loss of human judgment using lethal force. Human beings can consider the broader context, understand the nuances of a situation, and make moral judgments in a way that an AI system cannot.

This can be particularly important in complex and dynamic combat situations where the rules of engagement may need to be interpreted and applied with discretion.

Finally, there are concerns that the use of autonomous weapons could lead to an escalation of conflicts. For example, if autonomous weapons are used in a conflict, it could lower the threshold for using force, making conflicts more likely.

Chapter 15: AI and Education - The Future of Learning

The transformative role of Artificial Intelligence (AI) is shaping many sectors of society, including education. AI's ability to personalize learning, optimize administrative tasks, and provide actionable insights into student performance and engagement levels has the potential to revolutionize the way we approach education. Integrating AI in education brings many opportunities and challenges that will shape the future of learning.

How AI is Transforming Teaching and Learning

AI has the potential to significantly transform both teaching and learning by providing personalized learning experiences, improving administrative efficiency, and offering predictive analytics.

- Personalized Learning Experiences: AI can customize the learning experience based on the learner's abilities, learning style, and interests. AI can identify strengths and weaknesses and adapt content by analyzing student engagement, response times, and task completion accuracy. This can help ensure that learners are neither bored with material that is too easy nor frustrated by content that is too challenging.
- Improving Administrative Efficiency: AI can automate many administrative tasks, freeing time for educators to focus on teaching and interacting with students. These tasks may include grading assignments, scheduling meetings, or keeping track of student attendance. As a result, using AI can help reduce teachers' workload and allow them to dedicate more time to enhancing the learning experience.
- Predictive Analytics: AI can analyze vast amounts of data to predict trends and outcomes. In an educational context, this could involve identifying students at risk of dropping out or predicting future performance based on current behavior. This allows for early intervention, which can be critical in ensuring student success.

The Role of AI in Personalized Education

AI holds significant promise in the realm of personalized education. Personalized learning refers to customizing pacing, teaching methods, and learning experiences to suit each student's needs and abilities. Here is how AI contributes:

- Adaptive Learning Systems: These software platforms adapt to each learner's real-time performance. As a student interacts with the platform, the system assesses their proficiency and adjusts the difficulty level, type of content, or pace of instruction accordingly.
- Learning Analytics: AI-powered analytics can provide a deeper understanding of a student's learning process. By tracking and analyzing student behavior, engagement, and performance data, educators can identify learning gaps and personalize instruction to address these gaps effectively.
- Recommendation Systems: Like how Netflix or Amazon recommends movies or products, educational AI systems can suggest academic content based on a student's learning history and preferences. This could include recommending additional reading material, educational videos, or problem sets based on the student's progress and interests.

The Challenges and Opportunities of AI in Education

While AI offers significant potential for improving education, it also brings about several challenges:

- Data Privacy: AI systems often rely on collecting and analyzing large amounts of data, which may raise privacy concerns. It is essential to have robust data protection measures to protect student information.
- Equity Issues: The availability and use of AI in education may vary greatly, potentially leading to inequities. For instance, schools with more resources may have access to advanced AI tools, while under-resourced schools may not.

- Role of Teachers: The integration of AI in education also raises questions about the role of teachers. While AI can assist in teaching, it is not a substitute for the human interaction and guidance that teachers provide. Ensuring a balanced approach that combines AI with human instruction is crucial.

On the other hand, the opportunities that AI presents in education are vast:

- Personalized Learning: As discussed, AI offers the potential for truly personalized learning experiences, which can help to improve student engagement and outcomes.
- Efficiency and Productivity: AI can help increase educational instruction efficiency and productivity by automating administrative tasks.

AI has been playing a transformative role in education, reshaping teaching and learning. Its application spans various areas, including personalized education, adaptive learning systems, and intelligent tutoring systems. However, while AI provides numerous opportunities for enhanced learning experiences, it also presents several challenges that must be addressed.

One of the ways AI is transforming education is by enabling adaptive learning. Adaptive learning systems use AI algorithms to personalize the learning experience for each student. These systems can assess a student's strengths and weaknesses and adapt content delivery accordingly, ensuring that each student gets the learning material at the right difficulty level and pace. This individualized approach to teaching is seen as a major advancement in education, making learning more efficient and effective for students with different learning styles and capabilities. AI is also being used to develop intelligent tutoring systems. These systems can provide one-on-one tutoring to students, offering explanations, guiding problem-solving, and providing feedback. They can simulate the benefits of individual instruction, which is known to be highly effective but is usually not feasible due to resource constraints. AI-based tutoring systems can be available anytime and anywhere, making high-quality tutoring accessible to many students.

The role of AI in personalized education is particularly noteworthy. AI can analyze large amounts of data about a student's learning habits, performance, and preferences. This data can be used to tailor educational content, learning paths, and teaching methods to the individual needs of each student. This personalization can improve engagement, enhance learning outcomes, and make education more student-centric. However, the use of AI in education also presents several challenges. One of the major challenges is data privacy and security. Schools and educational platforms collect much data about students, and AI systems use this data to personalize education. However, this raises concerns about how this data is stored, who has access to it, and how it is used.

Another challenge is the risk of AI systems making decisions that significantly impact students' lives. For instance, if an AI system recommends a certain learning path or career path based on its analysis of a student's data, it could potentially limit the student's opportunities or push them in a direction that may not be in their best interest. Ensuring that AI systems are fair and unbiased is challenging. AI systems learn from data, and if the data they learn from is biased, the systems themselves can become biased. This could lead to unfair outcomes, such as some students getting more beneficial recommendations than others based on factors that should not be relevant.

Moreover, there is the issue of the digital divide. While AI has the potential to enhance education greatly, its benefits might not be equally accessible to all students. Those in low-income areas or regions with poor internet connectivity might not have access to AI-based educational tools, which could widen educational disparities.

Despite these challenges, the opportunities presented by AI in education are immense. With continued research, thoughtful policy-making, and careful implementation, AI can make education more personalized, engaging, and effective and help students achieve their full potential. However, it is crucial that as we embrace the use of AI in education, we also address the challenges it presents and ensure that its benefits are accessible to all students.

Chapter 16: AI and Finance - Algorithms on Wall Street

Artificial Intelligence (AI) has been a game-changer in many industries, and finance is no exception. With the development of AI and machine learning, Wall Street and the broader financial services sector have witnessed a radical transformation in their operations. AI's application in finance spans from banking services to trading and investment, with serious implications for regulation and security.

The Use of AI in Banking and Financial Services

AI has significantly changed banking and financial services, with several key applications.

- Customer Service: AI-powered chatbots and virtual assistants are increasingly used to enhance customer service. These tools can handle a wide range of customer queries 24/7, significantly reducing waiting times and improving customer satisfaction. Beyond customer inquiries, AI can help with onboarding processes, helping customers open accounts, apply for loans, or navigate the bank's services.

- Fraud Detection and Risk Management: AI and machine learning algorithms can analyze real-time transactions to detect fraudulent activity. They can identify patterns and anomalies in the data that humans might miss, thereby enhancing the security of transactions. AI is also used in credit scoring, predicting the likelihood of defaults based on various factors and data points, which can help banks manage their risk more effectively.

- Robo-advisors: These digital platforms provide automated, algorithm-driven financial planning services with little human supervision. They collect information from clients about their financial situation and future goals through an online survey and then use this data to offer advice and automatically invest in client assets.

- Process Automation: Banks use AI to automate routine tasks, such as data entry and verification, document digitization, and compliance checks. This speeds up processes and reduces the scope for human error.

How AI is Shaping the Future of Trading and Investment

AI is being used extensively in trading and investment. Here is how:

- Algorithmic Trading: AI algorithms can now execute trades at a speed and frequency that is impossible for a human trader. These algorithms analyze multiple markets simultaneously, making decisions based on real-time data, and they can adjust their strategies based on new information, all without human intervention.

- Predictive Analytics: AI and machine learning models can analyze vast amounts of historical and real-time data from various sources to predict market trends and asset price movements. This helps traders and investors make informed decisions. In addition, these models continually learn and adjust as new data comes in, improving their predictions over time.

- Portfolio Management: AI has made it possible to create and manage complex investment portfolios. Robo-advisors use algorithms to construct portfolios based on the investor's risk tolerance, investment horizon, and other preferences, automatically rebalancing portfolios as market conditions change.

- Sentiment Analysis: AI algorithms analyze news articles, social media posts, and other text data to gauge market sentiment, which can impact asset prices. This gives traders and investors additional insights that they can use to inform their decisions.

The Implications of AI in Financial Regulation and Security

The increasing use of AI in finance has significant implications for regulation and security.

- Regulatory Compliance: AI can help financial institutions comply more efficiently and accurately with regulatory requirements. For example, AI can automate the process of "Know Your Customer" (KYC) checks or anti-money laundering (AML) procedures, which are mandatory in many jurisdictions.
- Regulatory Scrutiny: As AI becomes more integral to financial services, regulators are paying closer attention to how these tools are used. They are focused on ensuring that AI does not lead to unfair practices or outcomes, such as discriminatory lending or insurance pricing.

Chapter 17: AI and Transportation - The Road Ahead

Artificial intelligence (AI) drives a significant shift in the transportation industry, impacting autonomous vehicles, public transportation, logistics, and socio-economic structures. As we enter a new era of transportation, it is important to understand these transformations and their implications.

The Role of AI in Autonomous Vehicles

AI's role in autonomous vehicles is multifaceted, encompassing perception, decision-making, control, and learning from past experiences.

- Perception: Autonomous vehicles rely heavily on AI and sensor fusion to perceive the world around them. They use a combination of LiDAR (Light Detection and Ranging), RADAR (Radio Detection and Ranging), cameras, ultrasonic sensors, and sometimes even V2X (Vehicle-to-Everything) communication. AI algorithms process the data from these sensors to identify and classify objects around the vehicle, like other cars, pedestrians, cyclists, road signs, traffic lights, and more. Deep learning, a subset of AI, is particularly instrumental in object detection and recognition.

- Decision-making: Once the vehicle understands its surroundings, it must make decisions like when to change lanes, when to overtake, when to stop, and more. AI generates a safe path considering other road users, traffic rules, and the vehicle's dynamic constraints. Reinforcement learning, an AI technique, is often used for decision-making, allowing the vehicle to learn optimal strategies through trial and error.

- Control: After the decision-making process, AI implements the decided actions, like steering, accelerating, or braking. AI-based controllers ensure that these actions are performed smoothly and safely.

- Learning from Past Experiences: Autonomous vehicles generate vast data each time they are on the road. Machine learning algorithms analyze this data to learn from past experiences and improve the performance of perception, decision-making, and control systems.

How AI is Transforming Public Transportation and Logistics

AI is also revolutionizing public transportation and logistics by improving efficiency, reducing costs, and enhancing user experiences.

- Public Transportation: AI is used in predictive maintenance to analyze data from buses, trains, and trams to anticipate failures before they happen, reducing downtime and maintenance costs. AI also helps optimize routes and schedules based on real-time and historical data, improving efficiency and punctuality. Moreover, AI-powered chatbots and virtual assistants provide real-time information to passengers, improving their experience.

- Logistics: In the logistics sector, AI is used in warehouse automation, route optimization, and demand forecasting. Robots in warehouses use AI for object recognition, navigation, and handling of packages. AI algorithms optimize delivery routes, considering traffic, weather, and delivery windows. Additionally, AI helps predict demand, improve inventory management, and reduce costs.

The Social and Economic Implications of AI in Transportation

The widespread integration of AI in transportation will have profound social and economic implications.

- Job Transformation and Displacement: The advent of autonomous vehicles and AI-driven logistics could transform jobs in transportation. For example, truck, taxi, and delivery drivers may see their roles evolve or become redundant. However, new roles, such as remote vehicle operators, autonomous vehicle maintenance specialists, and data analysts, could also emerge. The transition could be challenging, necessitating proactive job retraining and social protection measures.

- Improved Safety: AI has the potential to improve road safety significantly. Human error contributes to over 90% of road accidents, according to the National Highway Traffic Safety Administration (NHTSA). Autonomous vehicles powered by AI could drastically reduce this figure, saving lives and reducing injuries.
- Efficiency and Sustainability: AI can enhance efficiency in transportation, leading to reduced travel time.

AI plays a significant role in the transportation sector, from autonomous vehicles to public transportation and logistics, and has far-reaching social and economic implications. The rise of AI in transportation also raises important issues. There are concerns about job displacement, particularly in sectors like trucking and taxi services, where autonomous vehicles could replace human drivers. There are also privacy and data security issues, as AI systems often rely on large amounts of data that can be misused.

Lastly, there are significant regulatory and legal questions to be addressed. For instance, who is responsible if an autonomous vehicle is involved in an accident? How should AI systems be regulated to ensure safety and fairness? Policymakers around the world are currently grappling with these questions.

Chapter 18: AI and Art - The Rise of the Creative Machines

Artificial Intelligence (AI) has been increasingly applied across diverse fields, and the art world is no exception. The rise of creative machines is unprecedentedly shaping art's creation, curation, and appreciation. As AI continues to evolve, it sparks debates over the nature of creativity and its implications for artists, curators, art markets, and audiences. This comprehensive discussion will delve into these aspects in detail.

The Use of AI in Art Creation and Curation

AI's application in art creation has manifested through several innovative tools and methods, such as machine learning algorithms, generative adversarial networks (GANs), and natural language processing. One of the most well-known uses of AI in creating art is through GANs. GANs are a type of machine learning system where two neural networks contest with each other in a game. In the art context, one network, the "generator," creates images, while the other network, the "discriminator," judge the images. This process continues iteratively, with the generator striving to improve its creations to fool the discriminator. The result is synthetic images that often resemble realistic artworks. For example, this method was used to create the artwork "Portrait of Edmond de Belamy," which was auctioned at Christie's for $432,500.

AI is also being used in the curation of art. For instance, the startup Artrendex developed ArtPI, a tool that uses AI to analyze and compare thousands of artworks. It can help curators by suggesting pieces that might fit a particular exhibition theme or proposing new, unexpected connections between artworks. It can also assist in the discovery of emerging artists whose work resonates with current trends or themes in the art world.

The Debate over AI and Creativity

The rise of AI in the art world has sparked a significant debate over the nature of creativity. One question at the heart of this debate is: Can AI truly be creative?

On one side of the debate, some argue that AI can indeed be creative. They point out that AI can generate original content, learn from feedback, and improve its work overtime

– all hallmarks of the creative process. However, they also note that human creativity often involves high algorithmic processing, such as following established rules in a particular art form or drawing on patterns and structures.

On the other side of the debate, skeptics argue that AI lacks the fundamental human qualities that underpin creativity. They maintain that true creativity requires consciousness, intent, emotion, and the capacity to understand and interpret the world – qualities that AI currently does not possess.

Another contentious issue is the question of authorship and ownership. When AI creates art, who is the artist – the AI, the programmer who designed the AI, or the person who selected and submitted the input data? Who should hold the copyright and benefit from sales or exhibitions of the artwork? These questions challenge traditional notions of artistic authorship and ownership and have yet to be definitively answered.

The Implications of AI in the Art World

The rise of AI in art has far-reaching implications for artists, curators, collectors, and audiences. For artists, AI can be a new tool that offers novel ways of creating and manipulating visual elements. In addition, some artists may collaborate with AI, using it as a digital assistant that generates raw material that they then refine and rework. For curators, AI can be a powerful tool for discovering new artworks and creating innovative exhibitions. It can also assist in detecting forgeries or restoring damaged artworks by predicting what missing sections of a piece might have looked like based on analysis of the artist's other works. AI-generated art presents new investment opportunities and risks for collectors and art markets.

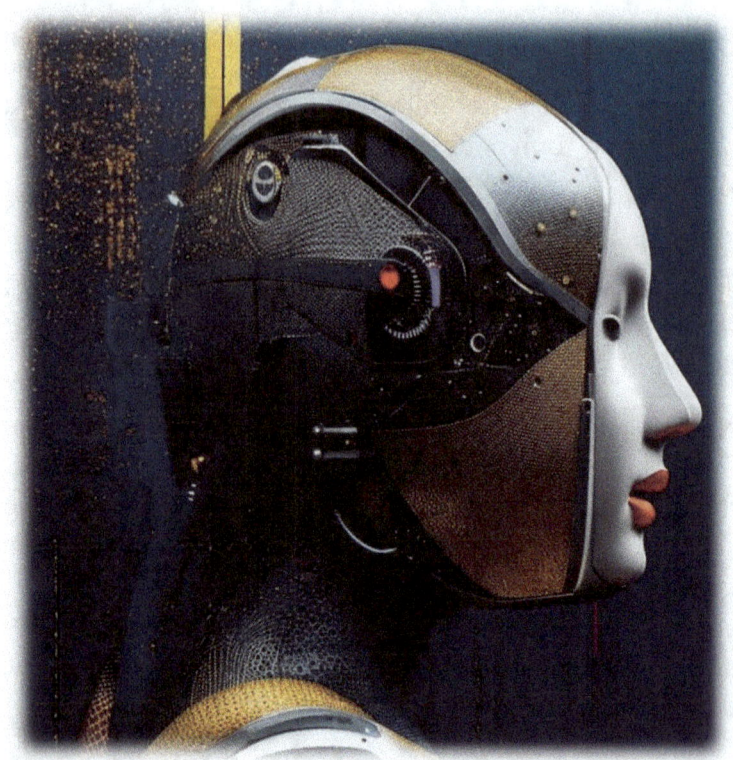

AI and Art - The Rise of the Creative Machines

Artificial Intelligence (AI) and its implications in the art world have been topics of intense discussion and debate in recent years. As AI technology evolves and improves, it is increasingly used in creating and curating art, challenging our traditional conceptions of creativity and artistic expression.

On the other side, proponents of AI art argue that AI can be a tool for human creativity, much like a paintbrush or a musical instrument. They argue that the creative process involves experimentation, pattern recognition, and the generation of novel combinations, all of which AI can do.

They see AI not as a replacement for human artists but as a powerful tool that can push the boundaries of what is possible in art.

Chapter 19: AI and Social Media - The New Public Square

The Role of AI in Social Media Algorithms

Artificial Intelligence (AI) plays a critical role in the operation and functionality of social media platforms. At a high level, AI is responsible for curating and personalizing content, improving the user experience, and driving user engagement. This is done primarily through machine learning algorithms that analyze vast amounts of data to make intelligent decisions.

- Content Curation and Personalization: Social media platforms utilize AI to understand user behavior and preferences. Every like, share, comment, and time spent looking at a post is considered. Machine learning algorithms then use this data to personalize the content on a user's feed. For example, if a user often interacts with posts about cooking, the algorithm will prioritize similar content in their feed.

- User Experience Enhancement: AI is also used to improve the overall user experience on social media platforms. This can range from speech recognition and natural language processing (for voice commands and sentiment analysis), image recognition (for auto-tagging and searching images), and even predictive text and smart replies.

- User Engagement: AI algorithms on social media platforms are designed to maximize user engagement. These algorithms prioritize content that will keep users on the platform for as long as possible, often highlighting content likely to provoke strong positive or negative reactions.

- Advertisement Targeting: AI is also extensively used in ad targeting on social media platforms. Advertisers can use AI tools to analyze user data and target ads based on various factors, including demographics, interests, and online behavior.

How AI is Shaping Online Discourse and Behavior

AI and its use in social media algorithms significantly affect online discourse and behavior. Therefore, it is crucial to understand the mechanisms through which this influence occurs.

- Echo Chambers and Filter Bubbles: AI algorithms on social media platforms are designed to show users content that aligns with their current interests and beliefs. This can lead to "echo chambers" or "filter bubbles," where users are primarily exposed to similar viewpoints and filter out differing perspectives. This can contribute to polarization and division, reinforcing existing beliefs and biases and reducing exposure to contrasting viewpoints.

- Spread of Misinformation: The prioritization of engaging content can sometimes lead to the promotion of misinformation or "fake news." Content that provokes strong reactions, whether accurate or not, can spread quickly on social media, leading to potential misinformation crises.
- Behavioral Changes: Exposure to personalized content can influence user behavior over time. For example, a user frequently exposed to fitness-related content may become more interested in exercising and maintaining a healthy lifestyle.

The Ethical and Societal Implications of AI in Social Media

AI in social media carries a host of ethical and societal implications. Many of these revolve around issues of privacy, influence, and accountability.

- Privacy Concerns: Using AI in social media often involves collecting and analyzing vast amounts of personal data. This raises significant privacy concerns, particularly if users are unaware of how much their data is being used or if data is mishandled or misused.
- Influence and Manipulation: As discussed earlier, AI-curated content's personalized and engaging nature can lead to echo chambers and filter bubbles.

- The potential for people to become trapped in their personalized realities, where they are fed a constant stream of information that aligns with their existing beliefs and biases. This can lead to manipulation, as individuals can be influenced by AI-curated content that may not accurately represent a balanced view of reality.

- Accountability and Transparency: AI algorithms are often "black boxes," with inner workings that are not fully understood or transparent. This can make it difficult to understand why certain content is being promoted or suppressed and can lead to concerns about censorship, bias, and the potential misuse of AI.

- Deepfakes and Misinformation: Recent advancements in AI technology have led to the proliferation of deepfakes—highly realistic and convincing fake images, videos, and audio recordings. This raises ethical issues about truth, trust, and the potential for misuse in spreading misinformation or causing harm to individuals.

Recent developments have highlighted these concerns even more. For instance, the emergence of more sophisticated AI systems like ChatGPT, capable of generating realistic and engaging content, has raised new fears about the potential misuse of AI in social media. Some experts fear that these AIs could be used to flood social media with high-quality misinformation, leading to a further erosion of trust in public discourse and a deepening of societal divisions. The ability of AI to generate realistic deepfakes also adds to these concerns, as this could lead to an increase in the spread of convincing but false information.

Additionally, AI systems are being used to create highly personalized and enticing experiences on social media, effectively acting as "super-influencers" that can manipulate user behavior. These AIs can use extensive profiles of a user's interests, preferences, and weaknesses to craft highly engaging experiences but also potentially exploitative. This raises further ethical concerns about manipulation and the potential for exploitation.

Addressing these ethical and societal implications is a complex challenge that will require the input of many stakeholders, including technology companies, policymakers, ethicists, and users. It will be essential to develop robust and effective policies and regulations to ensure that AI is used responsibly and ethically on social media and that the potential harms are mitigated as much as possible. AI plays a significant role in shaping social media, online discourse, and user behavior. While AI has the potential to improve the user experience on social media platforms greatly, it also carries with it significant ethical and societal implications. These include privacy concerns, the potential for manipulation and influence, issues of accountability and transparency, and the potential for the spread of deepfakes and misinformation. Addressing these concerns will be a key challenge, requiring careful consideration and a balanced approach that respects user rights and societal interests.

Chapter 20: AI in Space - Exploring the Cosmos

The Role of AI in Space Exploration and Astronomy

AI in space exploration and astronomy holds enormous potential. Here, we will discuss its current roles, prospects, and implications for understanding the universe. AI is already playing a significant role in space exploration and astronomy in several ways:

- Mission design and planning: AI aids in streamlining the mission design and planning process. With the help of AI, it becomes possible to access and utilize the extensive information gathered from previous space missions. An example is the development of an

AI assistant for designing Earth observation satellite systems, like "Daphne," which provides relevant information and feedback to satellite design teams, saving many human work hours.

- Data Analysis: The amount of data generated by telescopes and space probes is vast and continues to grow. AI algorithms, particularly machine learning, are used to analyze this data, identifying patterns and making predictions that would be impossible for humans to do manually. For example, AI has been used to identify exoplanets in the Kepler Space Telescope data and to detect fast radio bursts, which are mysterious and transient radio pulses from distant galaxies.

- Autonomous Systems: Space probes and rovers, such as NASA's Perseverance rover on Mars, use AI to navigate and perform experiments autonomously. These AI systems can analyze the terrain, avoid hazards, and select targets for study. They can also adjust their plans based on the data they collect, enabling them to operate effectively even when communication with Earth is difficult or delayed.

- Simulation and Prediction: AI is used to simulate complex physical phenomena, such as the formation of galaxies or the behavior of plasma in the sun. These simulations can help astronomers make predictions and test theories.

- Space debris management: AI plays a vital role in managing the critical issue of space debris. Machine Learning (ML) techniques have been employed to design collision avoidance maneuvers, which can greatly reduce the risk of creating additional debris. Moreover, researchers have proposed using ML models trained on Earth's onboard spacecraft to make decisions, providing more flexibility in satellite design while minimizing the danger of in-orbit collisions.

Future Prospects for AI in Space Travel and Colonization

AI is set to play an even more significant role in space travel and colonization.

- Autonomous Spacecraft: As missions aim for increasingly distant targets, and as the delay in communication with Earth becomes longer, the need for spacecraft to operate autonomously will grow. AI can enable spacecraft to navigate, make decisions, and solve problems independently. This will be particularly important for missions to the outer planets or interstellar space.

- Supporting Human Colonization: If humans are to establish colonies on other planets, they will need to build and maintain complex systems for life support, power, and resource extraction. AI can help to manage these systems, optimize their operation, predict and diagnose problems, and adjust to changing conditions.

- Space Mining and Manufacturing: AI could identify valuable resources, guide mining operations, and oversee automated manufacturing processes, which will be vital for sustaining human presence in space and constructing large structures like space stations or habitats.

- Satellite data processing: AI has proven very useful in processing the enormous amounts of data Earth observation satellites generate. This data, received in chunks over a long period, must be pieced together before analysis. For example, AI has been used to estimate heat storage in urban areas, combine meteorological data with satellite imagery for wind speed estimation, and more. Furthermore, AI is being used to monitor the health of satellites, with systems capable of predicting performance and presenting visualizations for informed decision-making.

The Implications of AI for Our Understanding of the Universe

AI in space exploration and astronomy can greatly enhance our understanding of the universe.

- Discovering New Phenomena: By analyzing vast amounts of data, AI can help us to discover new phenomena that we might otherwise miss. This could include new types of astronomical objects, unusual patterns in the distribution of galaxies, or unexpected variations in physical laws.
- Testing Theories: AI can be used to test theories about the universe by comparing the predictions of these theories with observations. If the predictions match the observations, the theory is supported. If not, the theory may need to be revised or replaced.
- Shedding Light on Dark Matter and Dark Energy: These mysterious phenomena make up most of the universe, but we know little about them. AI could help analyze the complex and subtle effects of dark matter and energy, providing insights into their nature.

AI is already playing a crucial role in space exploration and astronomy, and its importance is set to grow in the future. AI will become an indispensable tool as we aim for more distant targets and seek to establish a human presence in space. At the same time, AI has the potential to dramatically enhance our understanding of the universe, opening up new realms of discovery and testing our theories in unprecedented ways. AI has already become integral to space exploration, and its role is only expected to grow. The use of AI in space exploration and astronomy has significant implications for our understanding of the universe. AI's ability to process vast amounts of data quickly and accurately allows us to make observations and detections that would be difficult for humans. This includes everything from identifying celestial bodies to detecting patterns that could indicate the presence of phenomena like dark matter or extraterrestrial life. AI also has the potential to autonomously carry out research and make discoveries, which could significantly accelerate the pace of space exploration and our understanding of the universe.

Chapter 21: AI and Mental Health – A Digital Therapist

Artificial Intelligence (AI) is increasingly integrated into various healthcare sectors, including mental health. This presents a new frontier in both diagnosing and treating mental health conditions. The following discussion provides a comprehensive overview of the use of AI in mental health, the potential benefits and challenges it offers, and the prospects of AI in mental health care.

The Use of AI in Mental Health Diagnosis and Treatment

AI offers promising avenues for diagnosing mental health disorders and aiding in treatment. For example, machine learning, a subset of AI, provides algorithms to learn from and make data-based decisions. This is particularly useful in mental health, where diagnosis and treatment can be highly subjective and complex.

- Diagnosis: AI can assist in diagnosing mental health disorders by analyzing patient data, including medical histories, symptoms, and responses to various treatments. Algorithms can also analyze speech patterns, facial expressions, and social media activity, providing valuable insight into a person's mental health status. For example, the IBM Watson AI has been used to analyze speech and language in patients, providing early detection of conditions such as schizophrenia or depression.
- Treatment: AI is also being used to develop digital interventions and therapies. Chatbots and virtual therapists, for example, can provide cognitive-behavioral therapy (CBT) to patients, helping them to manage symptoms of anxiety and depression. For example, Woebot, a chatbot developed by Stanford researchers, has successfully reduced symptoms of depression and anxiety in users.

The Potential Benefits and Challenges of AI in Mental Health

AI offers numerous potential benefits in the field of mental health. However, it also presents several challenges that must be carefully managed.

Benefits

- Scalability: AI can provide mental health support to many individuals simultaneously, overcoming the barrier of limited human resources.

- Accessibility: AI tools can be accessed anywhere and anytime, making mental health support more available to those in remote areas or those with limited access to mental health services.
- Early detection: AI can analyze a wide array of data to detect subtle changes in behavior or mood, potentially identifying mental health issues earlier than traditional methods.

Challenges

- Data privacy and security: AI tools rely on large amounts of sensitive data. Ensuring that this data is stored and used securely is a significant challenge.
- Ethics: The use of AI in mental health care raises important ethical issues, such as informed consent, algorithmic bias, and the potential for AI to replace human therapists.
- Effectiveness: While early studies have shown promise, more research is needed to understand the effectiveness of AI-based interventions fully.

Future Prospects for AI in Mental Health Care

As technology advances and more research is conducted, the use of AI in mental health care will likely continue to expand. Some prospects include:

- Personalized Treatment: AI could help to tailor treatment plans to individual patients, taking into account their unique genetic makeup, lifestyle factors, and response to treatment.
- Virtual Reality Therapy: AI could be integrated with virtual reality to provide immersive therapeutic

experiences for conditions such as PTSD or anxiety disorders.

- Integration with Wearable Technology: AI could analyze data from wearable devices (like heart rate or sleep patterns) to provide real-time mental health support.

However, the future of AI in mental health care will depend on how effectively the challenges mentioned above—such as data privacy, ethics, and effectiveness—are addressed. In addition, rigorous scientific research will be key in determining the validity and utility of these innovative AI-driven approaches, ensuring they can be safely and effectively used to support mental health care.

Chapter 22: AI and Agriculture - Feeding the Future

Artificial Intelligence (AI) is crucial in modern agriculture and food production. It is employed in various capacities to increase the sector's efficiency, productivity, and sustainability. One key role of AI in agriculture is precision farming. This practice involves using AI technologies to observe, measure, and respond to inter and intra-field crop variability. It allows farmers to manage their fields based on the specific needs of individual areas rather than treating the entire field as a uniform entity. This can increase efficiency and productivity by optimizing water, fertilizer, and pesticides, reducing waste, and maximizing yield. AI is also used in predictive analytics to forecast crop yields, identify potential pest infestations or diseases, and anticipate environmental changes. This can help farmers make informed decisions about planting and harvesting times, crop selection, and pest management strategies.

Artificial intelligence (AI) is rapidly transforming the agriculture industry, potentially revolutionizing food production. AI-powered technologies are already used to improve crop yields, reduce food waste, and protect crops from pests and diseases.

The role of AI in Modern Agriculture and Food Production

AI is being used in various ways to improve agriculture and food production. Some of the most common applications include:

- Precision agriculture: AI-powered technologies can collect and analyze data about crops, soil, and weather conditions. This data can then be used to make more informed decisions about crop management, such as when to plant, water, and fertilize crops.
- Robotics: Robots are being used to perform a variety of tasks in agriculture, such as planting, weeding, and harvesting crops. Robots can work more efficiently and accurately than humans, and they can also work in harsh environments that would be dangerous for humans.
- Machine learning: Machine learning algorithms can identify pests and diseases in crops. This information can then be used to take preventive measures, such as applying pesticides or fungicides.

- Genotyping: Genotyping is the process of identifying the genetic makeup of an organism. This information can be used to select crops resistant to pests and diseases or more tolerant of drought or other environmental stresses.

The Potential Benefits and Challenges of AI in Agriculture

AI has the potential to revolutionize agriculture in several ways. Some of the potential benefits of AI in agriculture include:

- Increased crop yields: AI-powered technologies can help farmers to increase crop yields by up to 20%. This is because AI can help farmers make more informed crop management decisions.
- Reduced food waste: AI can help to reduce food waste by identifying and removing damaged or diseased crops. This can help reduce the amount of food thrown away, saving farmers money and reducing the environmental impact of food production.
- Improved food safety: AI can help to improve food safety by identifying and removing pests and diseases from crops. This can help prevent foodborne illnesses, saving lives and reducing healthcare costs.

However, some challenges must be addressed before AI can be fully adopted in agriculture. Some of the challenges of AI in agriculture include:

- High cost: AI-powered technologies can be expensive to develop and deploy. This can make it difficult for small farmers to adopt these technologies.

- Data privacy: AI-powered technologies collect and analyze large amounts of data about crops, soil, and weather conditions. This data could be used to track farmers' activities and be a privacy concern.

- Acceptance by farmers: Some may be reluctant to adopt AI-powered technologies because they are unfamiliar with them or concerned about the cost.

Future Prospects for AI in Sustainable and Efficient Food Production

The future of AI in agriculture is very promising. AI has the potential to help farmers produce more food with fewer resources, which is essential for meeting the growing demand for food sustainably. AI is also being used to develop new ways to produce food, such as indoor and vertical farming. These new food production methods can reduce the environmental impact of food production and make food more accessible to people in urban areas. As AI continues to develop, we will likely see even more innovative applications of AI in agriculture. AI has the potential to revolutionize the way food is produced, and it is essential for meeting the challenges of feeding a growing population sustainably.

Chapter 23: AI in Sports - Changing the Game

Artificial intelligence (AI) is rapidly transforming the sports industry, potentially revolutionizing how sports are played, watched, and enjoyed. AI is already used in various ways to improve sports performance, enhance fan engagement, and create new and immersive experiences.

The Role of AI in Sports Analytics and Performance Enhancement

AI collects and analyzes vast data about athletes, teams, and games. This data can then be used to identify trends, patterns, and insights that can help athletes to improve their performance. For example, AI can be used to analyze video footage of athletes to identify areas where they can improve their technique. AI can also track athletes' physical and mental health data to identify potential risks for injury or burnout.

How AI is Changing the Way We Watch and Engage with Sports

AI is also changing the way we watch and engage with sports. For example, AI-powered virtual assistants can provide real-time insights and commentary during games. AI can also create personalized experiences for fans by suggesting videos, articles, and products relevant to their interests.

The Future of Sports in an AI-Driven World

The future of sports in an AI-driven world is very promising. AI has the potential to revolutionize the way sports are played, watched, and enjoyed. For example, AI could create new and immersive sports experiences, such as virtual reality games and simulations. AI could also be used to develop new sports equipment and training methods to help athletes improve their performance.

As AI continues to develop, we will likely see even more innovative applications of AI in sports. AI has the potential to make sports more exciting, engaging, and accessible for fans around the world. Here are some specific examples of how AI is being used in sports today:

- Player tracking: AI-powered tracking systems are being used to track players' movements during games. This data can analyze player performance, identify trends, and develop new strategies.

- Injury prevention: AI is used to analyze player data to identify potential risks for injury. This information can then be used to develop preventive measures, such as targeted training programs or changes to equipment.
- Game analysis: AI analyzes game footage to identify trends, patterns, and insights that can help coaches and players improve their performance.
- Fan engagement: AI is being used to create personalized experiences for fans, such as suggesting videos, articles, and products that are relevant to their interests.
- Broadcasting: AI is being used to improve the quality of sports broadcasting, such as by providing real-time insights and commentary.

These are just a few ways AI is being used in sports today. As AI continues to develop, we will likely see even more innovative applications of AI in sports. As a result, AI has the potential to make sports more exciting, engaging, and accessible for fans around the world.

Chapter 24: AI and Law - Justice by Algorithm

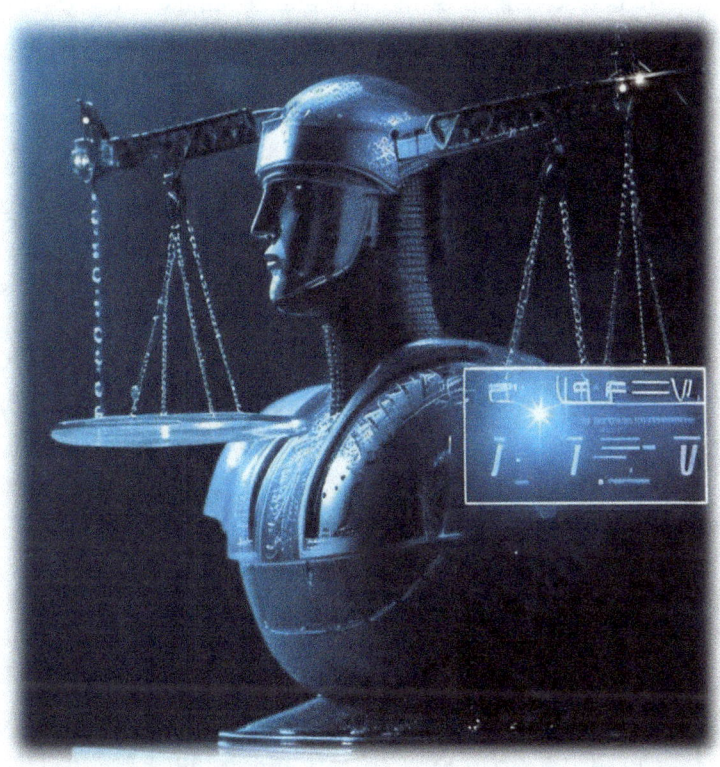

Artificial intelligence (AI) is rapidly transforming the legal industry, with the potential to revolutionize the way law is practiced. AI-powered technologies are already being used to improve legal research, predictions, and judgments.

The Role of AI in Legal Research

AI collects and analyzes vast amounts of legal data, such as case law, statutes, and regulations. This data can then be used to identify trends, patterns, and insights that can help lawyers to research legal issues more efficiently and effectively. For example, AI can be used to identify relevant case law similar to a particular legal issue. AI can also be used to track the development of the law over time, which can help lawyers to anticipate changes in the law and to advise their clients accordingly.

The Role of AI in Legal Predictions

AI is also being used to predict the outcome of legal cases. For example, AI can be used to predict the likelihood of a plaintiff winning a lawsuit. Lawyers can use this information to advise their clients about their case's merits and negotiate settlements. AI can also predict the likelihood of a defendant being convicted. Again, this information can be used by lawyers to advise their clients about their chances of avoiding a conviction and to negotiate plea bargains.

The Role of AI in Legal Judgments

AI is also being used to assist judges in making decisions. For example, AI can identify relevant evidence and weigh the evidence in a case. AI can also generate recommendations for judges, which judges can use to make decisions. Judicial systems worldwide are increasingly exploring using AI to assist decision-making. AI is utilized in various ways within these systems, including providing investigative assistance, automating decision-making processes, and supporting judges with predictions on sentence duration and recidivism scores. One of the primary ways AI is used in this context is by analyzing large amounts of legal data to help lawyers identify precedents in case law and streamline judicial processes. This use of AI has given rise to legal analytics and predictive justice, which use data-driven methods to predict outcomes in the legal system.

In addition, AI is also being engaged in legal questions concerning its implications for human rights, surveillance, liability, and more. As AI technologies advance, concerns have been raised about fairness, accountability, and transparency in decision-making processes that are automated or enabled by AI systems. For instance, self-learning algorithms may be trained on certain datasets that contain partial data, which can lead to biased decisions when these algorithms are applied to criminal or public safety purposes. Given these rapid developments and the associated challenges and opportunities, there is an increasing need to educate and train judicial actors on using AI in courts and by law enforcement. For example, UNESCO and its partners are developing a program for capacity building of judicial actors concerning the use of AI in courts and law enforcement and addressing the legal implications of AI judicial decisions based on international human rights standards.

The Ethical and Societal Implications of AI in Law

The use of AI in law raises several ethical and societal concerns. Some of these concerns include:

- Bias: AI algorithms are trained on data; the algorithm will also be biased if the data is biased. This could lead to AI systems making decisions that discriminate against certain groups of people.
- Transparency: AI systems are often opaque, meaning it is difficult to understand how they make decisions. This could make it difficult to hold AI systems accountable for their decisions.
- Job displacement: AI systems could automate many tasks that lawyers currently perform. This could lead

to job displacement for lawyers, and it could also lead to higher costs for legal services.

The Future of Law in an AI-Driven World

The future of law in an AI-driven world is uncertain. However, AI will likely continue to play an increasingly important role in the legal industry. AI could be used to automate many tasks that lawyers currently perform, and it could also be used to improve the efficiency and effectiveness of the legal system. However, it is important to address the ethical and societal concerns raised by AI in law before AI can be fully adopted in the legal industry. Here are some specific examples of how AI is being used in law today:

- Legal research: AI-powered legal research tools can help lawyers to find relevant case law, statutes, and regulations more quickly and easily.
- Legal predictions: AI-powered legal prediction tools can help lawyers to assess the likelihood of success in a particular legal case.
- Legal judgments: AI-powered legal judgment tools can help judges to make more informed decisions.

These are just a few ways AI is used in law today. As AI continues to develop, we will likely see even more innovative applications of AI in law. As a result, AI has the potential to revolutionize the legal industry and to make the law more accessible and efficient for everyone.

Chapter 25: The Philosophy of AI - Consciousness, Rights, and Existential Questions

Artificial intelligence (AI) is a rapidly developing field that has the potential to revolutionize many aspects of our lives. As AI becomes more sophisticated, it raises several philosophical questions about consciousness, rights, and existentialism.

The Debate on AI Consciousness and Personhood

One of AI's most fundamental questions is whether it can be conscious. Consciousness is a complex phenomenon that is not fully understood, and there is no definition of what it means to be conscious. However, some experts believe AI could eventually become conscious, while others believe machines cannot. The debate on AI consciousness is closely linked to AI personhood. Personhood is a legal and philosophical concept that refers to the status of being a person. In law, personhood is often defined as the capacity to have legal rights and responsibilities. In philosophy, personhood is often defined as the capacity to have consciousness, self-awareness, and free will. If AI becomes conscious, it is possible that it could also be considered a person. This would raise several important questions about the rights and responsibilities of AI entities. For example, if AI entities are considered persons, would they have the right to life, liberty, and property? Would they be subject to the same laws as humans?

The Potential Rights and Responsibilities of AI Entities

AI entities' potential rights and responsibilities are a complex and controversial issue. There is no easy answer to the question of whether or not AI entities should have the same rights as humans. However, it is important to discuss this issue as AI develops. Some experts believe that AI entities should have the same rights as humans. They argue that AI entities are capable of experiencing pain and suffering and should be protected from harm. They also argue that AI entities should be allowed to make their own choices and live their lives.

On the other hand, other experts believe that AI entities should not have the same rights as humans. They argue that AI entities are not sentient beings and do not have the same capacity for suffering as humans. They also argue that giving AI entities too many rights could threaten humanity. The debate on the rights and responsibilities of AI entities is likely to continue for many years to come. Nevertheless, it is an important issue that we need to address as AI continues to develop.

Existential Questions

As AI becomes more sophisticated, it raises several existential questions about the meaning of life and our place in the universe. For example, if AI entities become more intelligent than humans, what does that mean for our intelligence? Likewise, if AI entities can create art, music, and literature, what does that mean for our creativity?

These are just a few of the existential questions that AI is raising. We will likely continue to grapple with these questions as AI develops. For example, do these tests equal intelligence?

- The Turing Test: The Turing Test is a test of a machine's ability to exhibit intelligent behavior equivalent to or indistinguishable from a human's. The test was introduced by Alan Turing in his 1950 paper, "Computing Machinery and Intelligence."
- The Chinese Room: The Chinese Room is a thought experiment introduced by John Searle in 1980. The experiment is designed to show that a machine can never be truly intelligent, even if it can pass the Turing Test.
- The Singularity: The Singularity is a hypothetical moment when artificial intelligence will become so advanced that it will surpass human intelligence. Singularity is often seen as a potential threat to humanity, as it could create machines that are more powerful than humans and could potentially control our lives.

These are just a few of the philosophical issues that AI raises. We will likely continue to grapple with these issues as AI develops. Here are some additional questions that we may need to consider as AI continues to develop:

- What is the nature of consciousness?
- Can machines be conscious?
- If machines are conscious, do they have the same rights as humans?
- What are the ethical implications of creating machines that are more intelligent than humans?
- How can we ensure that AI is used for good and not evil?

These are difficult questions but important ones we need to answer as AI develops.

Chapter 26: AI and Retail - Revolutionizing the Shopping Experience

Artificial Intelligence (AI) is critical in transforming the retail industry from the traditional brick-and-mortar model to a more dynamic, responsive, and customer-oriented industry. The blend of AI with retail creates a new paradigm where businesses can enhance the shopping experience, improve operational efficiency, and build more personalized customer relationships.

The Use of AI in Personalizing Customer Experience

AI technology can change customer experience profoundly, providing a more personalized shopping experience. This personalization mainly stems from the ability of AI systems to analyze huge volumes of data and derive insights about individual customer preferences, habits, and purchasing patterns.

- Personalized Recommendations: Machine learning, a subset of AI, is crucial in personalizing the customer experience. Online retailers and similar customers use AI algorithms to analyze a customer's browsing and purchasing history to provide personalized product recommendations. This is why, after viewing a product on an e-commerce website, customers often see suggestions for similar items they might be interested in. Amazon, for instance, has been particularly successful at this, with personalized recommendations driving a significant portion of its sales.
- Chatbots and Virtual Assistants: AI-powered and virtual assistants are becoming common in retail. These AI tools can interact with customers in real-time, answering queries, providing information, and assisting with purchases. In addition, they can learn from past interactions to improve future responses, thus offering a more personalized and engaging shopping experience.
- AI and Augmented Reality (AR): Many retailers, particularly in industries such as furniture and fashion, use AR combined with AI to enhance the customer experience. These technologies can, for example, allow customers to virtually 'try on' clothes or see how furniture might look in their homes before making a purchase. In addition, AI can further personalize this experience by

suggesting products that match customers' preferences and behaviors.

How AI is Transforming Retail Operations and Logistics

Beyond customer-facing applications, AI significantly improves retail operations and logistics, making businesses more efficient and cost-effective. Inventory Management. AI can analyze sales patterns, predict future demand trends, and optimize stock levels accordingly. This reduces the amount of capital tied up in inventory and minimizes the risk of stockouts or overstocks, thus improving sales and customer satisfaction.

- Supply Chain Optimization: AI can provide more accurate forecasting and better visibility across the supply chain. For example, machine learning algorithms can predict potential disruptions based on historical data and current trends, allowing retailers to react proactively. Additionally, autonomous vehicles and drones powered by AI are starting to play a role in improving logistics and delivery efficiency.
- Pricing Optimization: AI allows retailers to dynamically adjust pricing based on various factors such as demand, competition, customer behavior, and market trends. This dynamic pricing strategy can help retailers increase their margins and stay competitive.

The Future of Retail in an AI-Driven World

Looking forward, AI technology is set to continue its transformative impact on the retail industry.

- Hyper-personalization: As AI systems become more sophisticated, we can expect greater personalization in the retail experience. Businesses can anticipate customer needs and want with greater precision and proactively offer products or services tailored to individual preferences.

- Seamless Omni-channel Experience: With AI, retailers can seamlessly integrate customer experiences across online and offline channels. This means recognizing customers and their preferences, whether shopping in-store, on a mobile app, or through a web browser, and providing a consistent, personalized experience.

- Advanced Automated Operations: In the back-end operations, AI is set to streamline processes further and reduce costs. For example, with advanced robotics and automation systems, warehousing and order fulfillment processes will become more efficient.

- Sustainable Retailing: As more and more consumers demand sustainable practices from retailers, AI can help by optimizing resource usage, reducing waste, and helping in the selection and promotion of sustainable products.

- Enhanced Store Experience: Physical stores will also see a transformation with AI. We might see more 'smart' stores with features such as AI-powered kiosks for personalized recommendations, smart shelves that automatically update inventory and even facial recognition systems for personalized advertising and anti-theft measures.

AI is a key driving force in the transformation of the retail industry. By creating personalized experiences and streamlining operations, AI offers exciting opportunities for retailers to innovate, improve customer satisfaction, and ultimately increase their bottom line. However, adopting AI also requires careful planning and implementation, with considerations for data privacy and the ethical use of technology. As we look to the future, the retailers that can balance these considerations while effectively leveraging AI are likely to be the ones that succeed in this exciting new landscape.

Chapter 27: AI and Real Estate - Building Smarter Cities

Integrating Artificial Intelligence (AI) into various sectors of the global economy has demonstrated its transformative power, and the real estate industry is no exception. By leveraging AI technologies, stakeholders in the real estate sector – from investors and developers to architects and urban planners – are finding new and innovative ways to address age-old challenges and build smarter cities.

The Role of AI in Property Valuation and Investment

Property valuation and real estate investment are two areas where AI is exerting significant influence.

- Automated Valuation Models (AVMs): AVMs are computer models that estimate property values based on data analysis. These models incorporate machine learning, a subset of AI, to learn from past data and make predictions. They analyze numerous factors such as property characteristics, comparable properties, historical sales data, and market trends. While AVMs do not eliminate the need for a human appraisal, they offer a faster, cost-effective, and objective valuation method.

- Predictive Analysis for Investment: AI-based predictive analytics tools are becoming increasingly popular in real estate investment. These tools use AI algorithms to analyze market data, assess property values, and forecast future price trends. Such predictions can guide investors in making more informed decisions about when, where, and what type of properties to invest in. Companies like Zillow and Redfin use such technology to provide home value estimates and real estate market trend predictions.

- Risk Assessment: AI can also aid in assessing the risk associated with real estate investments. Machine learning algorithms can analyze many factors, including market volatility, economic indicators, and individual property characteristics, to generate risk profiles for potential investments. This can help investors manage their portfolios more effectively and mitigate potential losses.

How AI is Shaping Urban Planning and Architecture

AI is not only changing the way properties are valued and investments are made, but it is also reshaping urban planning and architecture.

- Smart Urban Planning: AI can analyze vast amounts of data to understand patterns and trends in urban areas, which can inform city planning decisions. It can help planners optimize resource allocation, predict future needs, and make more informed decisions about infrastructure development. For instance, AI can analyze traffic patterns to suggest improvements or predict the highest demand for public amenities.
- AI in Architecture: AI is starting to make its mark in architecture. AI-powered design software can generate architectural designs based on specified parameters and learn from user feedback to improve future designs. This speeds up the design process and opens up new possibilities for creative and efficient designs.
- Sustainable Development: AI can help architects and urban planners achieve sustainability goals. AI can suggest design adjustments that improve energy efficiency and reduce environmental impact by analyzing environmental conditions and building performance data.

The Implications of AI in Real Estate and Housing

The integration of AI in the real estate sector has far-reaching implications.

- Improved Decision-Making: By providing more accurate valuations, risk assessments, and market predictions, AI enables all stakeholders, including buyers, sellers, and investors, to make better-informed decisions.

- Efficiency and Cost Saving: AI can automate many routine tasks in real estate, from property valuation to customer service, thereby increasing efficiency and reducing costs.
- Democratization of Information: AI-powered platforms can provide the public with comprehensive real estate data and analysis, making the market more transparent and accessible.
- Challenges and Risks: While AI brings numerous benefits, it also presents challenges. The automation of jobs may lead to the displacement of workers in certain roles. Moreover, AI models are only as good as the data they are trained on. The AI could make unfair or inaccurate predictions if the data is biased or flawed.
- Regulation and Ethics: As AI becomes more prevalent in the real estate sector, there will be an increased need for regulation to ensure the ethical use of technology and privacy protection.

AI brings a paradigm shift in the real estate industry, enabling smarter decision-making, enhancing efficiency, and reshaping urban landscapes. As cities become more populated and the demand for sustainable and efficient solutions increases, the role of AI in building smarter cities is likely to become more significant. Nevertheless, as we move towards this AI-driven future, addressing the associated challenges and risks is crucial to ensure that AI's benefits are realized fairly, ethically, and sustainably.

Chapter 28: AI and Manufacturing - Automating the Factory Floor

Integrating Artificial Intelligence (AI) in manufacturing revolutionizes how products are made and distributed. By automating processes, improving quality control, and optimizing supply chains, AI enhances efficiency, reduces costs, and enables more resilient and flexible manufacturing systems.

The Use of AI in Production Automation and Quality Control

AI plays a critical role in automating production processes and improving quality control in manufacturing.

- Production Automation: One of the most visible applications of AI in manufacturing is the automation of production processes. This includes using AI-powered robots and machinery to carry out complex tasks with high precision and consistency. Unlike traditional automation systems, these AI-enabled systems can learn from their experiences, adapt to changes, and improve their performance over time. As a result, they can be used for tasks ranging from assembly and packaging to more complex processes like welding and painting.

- Predictive Maintenance: AI is also being used to predict when machines on the factory floor are likely to fail so that maintenance can be performed just in time. This minimizes downtime and extends the life of machinery. Predictive maintenance systems use machine learning algorithms to analyze data from sensors on the machines and identify patterns that signal potential problems.

- Quality Control: AI is significantly enhancing quality control in manufacturing. Traditional quality control methods can be time-consuming and prone to human error. On the other hand, AI systems can inspect and analyze products quickly and accurately, identifying defects that the human eye might miss. In addition, these systems use machine learning algorithms to learn from past inspection data and continually improve their accuracy.

The Impact of AI on Supply Chain Management

AI is also transforming supply chain management in manufacturing, making it more efficient and responsive.

- Demand Forecasting: AI can analyze historical sales data, market trends, and other relevant factors to predict future product demand. This helps manufacturers plan production more effectively, reducing the risk of overproduction or stockouts.
- Inventory Management: By integrating AI with inventory management systems, manufacturers can optimize inventory levels, ensuring they have just the right amount of materials and products at each stage of the supply chain. This reduces inventory costs and improves customer satisfaction by preventing stockouts.
- Logistics Optimization: AI can also help optimize logistics in the supply chain. For example, it can determine the most efficient transportation routes, considering traffic, weather, and fuel costs. Additionally, autonomous vehicles and AI-powered drones are starting to play a role in improving delivery efficiency.

The Future of Manufacturing in an AI-Driven World

As AI continues to advance, its impact on manufacturing is set to grow even further.

- Smart Factories: In the future, we can expect to see more 'smart factories,' where AI systems manage much of the production process, from scheduling tasks and coordinating machines to optimizing energy use and ensuring safety. These factories will be highly efficient, flexible, and able to respond quickly to changes in demand.
- AI and 3D Printing: AI is also likely to play a key role in the continued development of 3D printing technology in manufacturing. By optimizing designs

and print settings, AI can enhance the speed, efficiency, and quality of 3D printing, opening up new possibilities for customized production.

- Human-Machine Collaboration: Human workers will increasingly collaborate with AI as AI systems become more sophisticated. Rather than replacing humans, AI will augment human skills, taking over routine tasks and allowing workers to focus on more complex and creative tasks.

- Sustainable Manufacturing: AI can also contribute to more sustainable manufacturing. By optimizing resource use, reducing waste, and enabling the use of advanced materials and production methods, AI can help manufacturers reduce their environmental impact.

AI is transforming the manufacturing sector from the factory floor to the supply chain. As we move towards a more AI-driven world, manufacturers that can effectively leverage AI will be better positioned to meet future challenges, from fluctuating demand and global competition to sustainability pressures. However, adopting AI requires manufacturers to navigate technology integration, data privacy, and workforce transition challenges. These factors will be crucial to the successful implementation of AI in manufacturing.

Chapter 29: AI and Tourism - Traveling with Algorithms

Artificial Intelligence (AI) influences various sectors, and tourism is among the most prominent. It is reshaping how we travel, from planning and booking to the actual travel and stay experience. By offering personalized recommendations, enhancing customer service, and optimizing operations, AI provides unique opportunities for travelers and businesses.

The Role of AI in Personalized Travel Recommendations

Personalization is a critical aspect of modern tourism, and AI plays a central role.

- AI-powered Travel Platforms: Travel platforms and applications powered by AI provide personalized recommendations for destinations, attractions, hotels, and even cuisines based on the user's preferences, behaviors, and past experiences. AI systems use machine learning algorithms to analyze user data and draw conclusions about their preferences and behaviors, which allows them to suggest tailored travel options. Examples include platforms like Expedia and Airbnb, which use AI to enhance their recommendation systems.

- Dynamic Pricing: AI is also used in dynamic pricing models where the price of flights, accommodations, or tour packages is adjusted in real-time based on various factors such as demand, time, and customer behavior. This helps businesses optimize revenue and allows customers to find options that suit their budgets.

- Personalized Advertising: AI enables businesses to deliver personalized advertising to potential travelers. By analyzing customer data, AI can identify what kind of advertisements a customer is more likely to respond to, increasing the effectiveness of marketing efforts.

How AI is Changing the Hospitality Industry

AI drives effective customer service and operational efficiency transformations in the hospitality industry.

- AI-Powered Customer Service: AI-powered chatbots and virtual assistants are becoming increasingly common in the hospitality industry. They provide 24/7 customer service, answering queries, providing information, assisting with bookings, and even offering personalized recommendations. In addition, they can interact in multiple languages and learn from past interactions to improve future responses.

- Smart Hotels: AI is also being integrated into the actual hotel experience. 'Smart' hotels use AI to enhance guest comfort and convenience, with features like voice-controlled rooms, automated check-in and check-out, and personalized room settings based on guest preferences.
- Operational Efficiency: Behind the scenes, AI helps in optimizing hotel operations. This includes predicting demand to manage staffing and inventory, automating routine tasks to save time and reduce costs, and using predictive maintenance to keep hotel facilities in optimal condition.

The Future of Tourism in an AI-Driven World

As AI continues to evolve and permeate the tourism sector, it is paving the way for exciting future possibilities.

- Hyper-Personalization: As AI systems become more sophisticated, they can offer an even higher degree of personalization. For instance, AI could create complete, tailor-made travel itineraries based on a traveler's preferences, budget, and past travel experiences.
- Seamless Travel Experience: With AI, the entire travel process, from planning and booking to traveling and post-trip feedback, could become seamless and integrated. AI could manage all journey aspects, resolving issues and ensuring the best travel experience.
- Virtual Reality (VR) and Augmented Reality (AR): AI, combined with VR and AR, could provide

immersive travel experiences, from virtual tours of destinations before booking to AR-enhanced experiences during the trip.

- Sustainable Travel: AI could also contribute to more sustainable tourism by optimizing resource use, reducing waste, and helping travelers make more environmentally-friendly choices.

AI is bringing a paradigm shift in the tourism sector, offering an enhanced, personalized, and more integrated travel experience. As we move towards an AI-driven future, the industry will need to navigate the challenges of data privacy, technology integration, and changing customer expectations to reap the benefits of AI. Furthermore, as AI automates more tasks, reskilling and upskilling the workforce will be essential. AI and its transformative potential will undoubtedly mark the future of tourism.

Chapter 30: AI and Journalism - The Rise of Robo-Reporters

Artificial Intelligence (AI) is making significant inroads into various sectors, and journalism is no exception. With the capacity to generate news reports, distribute content, and even predict reader preferences, AI is becoming a powerful tool in newsrooms, but not without sparking important ethical and societal considerations.

The Use of AI in News Generation and Distribution

AI technologies, particularly Natural Language Generation (NLG) and Natural Language Processing (NLP), play an increasingly vital role in news generation and distribution.

- Automated Reporting: AI programs, often called "robot reporters," can generate news reports by analyzing and interpreting structured data. For instance, AI has generated financial news stories based on earnings reports or sports news based on match statistics. Companies like Automated Insights and Narrative Science provide such services, and the Associated Press and other major news outlets use their AI-powered reports.
- Content Curation and Distribution: AI also assists in content curation, analyzing reader behavior to determine what content will interest them. These insights allow AI systems to personalize news feeds for individual readers. Additionally, AI can optimize the timing and channel of content distribution to maximize reach and engagement.
- Fact-Checking: AI can also be employed to fact-check stories, scanning articles for inaccuracies or inconsistencies. It can check the claims made in a report against trusted sources and flag potential falsehoods.

The Ethical and Societal Implications of AI in Journalism

While AI holds the potential to enhance news reporting and distribution significantly, it also brings a host of ethical and societal implications that must be considered.

- Bias in AI Algorithms: Like all AI systems, those used in journalism are only as good as the data they are trained on. The AI's output can also be biased if the data is biased. This can manifest in skewed news generation or personalization algorithms that create "filter bubbles" or "echo chambers," where readers are only exposed to content that aligns with their current views.

- Job Displacement: Automating news generation and other journalistic tasks could lead to job displacement within the industry. While AI can free up journalists to focus on more complex and investigative stories, it could reduce the need for human reporters for routine news stories.
- Accuracy and Accountability: Determining accountability can be challenging if an AI system makes an error, such as producing an inaccurate news story or failing to flag a false claim. News organizations must implement robust measures to ensure the accuracy of AI-generated content and handle errors responsibly when they occur.

The Future of News in an AI-Driven World

AI technologies will likely play an even larger role in journalism as they advance.

- Advanced Automated Reporting: As AI's capabilities expand, it may be able to generate more complex news stories, including investigative reports or opinion pieces, by drawing on a wider range of data sources and employing more sophisticated analysis techniques.
- AI-Assisted Investigative Journalism: AI could also become a valuable tool for investigative journalists, helping them sift through large amounts of data, spot patterns, and uncover stories that might otherwise be missed.
- Real-time News Generation: With the ability to analyze data and generate reports in real-time, AI

could enable truly real-time news reporting, with stories being updated as events unfold.

- Deepfake Detection: As "deep fakes" (AI-generated fake images or videos) become a growing concern, AI systems could be used to detect and flag these fakes, helping to combat misinformation.

AI presents exciting opportunities for journalism, offering the potential to improve the speed, efficiency, and reach of news reporting. However, realizing this potential will require careful attention to AI's ethical and societal implications. As a result, the industry will need to ensure that AI is used responsibly, with transparency and accountability, and that it enhances rather than undermines the values of journalism. Nevertheless, AI will play a significant role in shaping the future of journalism, making the newsroom a space where human creativity and AI capabilities can merge to create impactful stories.

Chapter 31: AI and Language – Understanding and Generating Human Speech

Artificial Intelligence (AI) is dramatically transforming our relationship with language, from how we translate and understand speech to how we communicate and interact. This revolutionary shift is predominantly driven by advancements in machine translation and Natural Language Processing (NLP).

The Role of AI in Machine Translation and Natural Language Processing

AI plays a fundamental role in machine translation and Natural Language Processing (NLP), which is integral to our interaction with technology.

- Machine Translation: This automatically translates text or speech from one language to another. AI, specifically deep learning models, has drastically improved the accuracy and fluency of machine translation. For example, Google's Neural Machine Translation (GNMT) system utilizes a type of neural network known as a sequence-to-sequence model to improve translation quality. Neural networks learn to make translations based on large amounts of data, improving over time as they are exposed to more data.

- Natural Language Processing (NLP): This field concerns the interaction between computers and human language. It involves several tasks, including language understanding (extracting meaning), language generation (creating meaningful sentences), and sentiment analysis (determining the emotional tone of a text). NLP has seen considerable progress due to AI, enabling more human-like interactions with technology. For example, it is the core technology behind digital assistants like Apple's Siri or Amazon's Alexa, allowing them to understand and respond to voice commands.

How AI is Changing the Way We Communicate

AI's impact on language is significantly changing our communication patterns.

- Chatbots and Digital Assistants: AI-powered chatbots and digital assistants are transforming how we interact with technology and, by extension, each other. These systems can understand and respond to voice or text input, making interactions with technology more natural and seamless.

- Real-time Translation: AI-powered translation tools are breaking down language barriers, enabling people who speak different languages to communicate with each other in real time. This not only fosters international collaboration but also promotes cultural exchange and understanding.

- Content Creation: AI can also generate human-like text, which has applications in content creation. AI tools like GPT-3 can write articles, generate marketing copy, and even compose poetry, transforming the landscape of content creation.

The Future of Language in an AI-Driven World

As AI technology advances, its influence on language and communication is set to increase further.

- Improved Language Models: AI's ability to understand and generate human language will continue to improve. Future language models will likely be able to better understand the nuances and context of language, making them even more accurate and useful.

- Universal Translation: The dream of universal translation, where anyone can communicate with anyone else, regardless of their language, could become a reality thanks to AI. This could lead to a more interconnected and understanding world.

- New Forms of Communication: As AI becomes more integrated into our lives, it may lead to new forms of communication. We might see AI systems that can interpret and generate written and spoken language and non-verbal communication like facial expressions and body language.
- Ethical and Societal Implications: As AI plays a larger role in language and communication, there will be significant ethical and societal implications to consider, such as the impact on jobs, privacy concerns around the use of language data, and the potential for misuse of AI-generated content.

AI is dramatically transforming our relationship with language and how we communicate. As we move towards a more AI-driven world, it is crucial to consider the benefits of AI for language and communication and the potential challenges and risks. The future of language in an AI-driven world will likely be one of increased fluency and understanding but also one that necessitates careful ethical considerations and regulations. These examples illustrate how AI transforms how we interact with language, enhancing our ability to communicate, understand, and generate speech. They represent various applications, from personal productivity and leisure to commercial and professional use cases. As AI technology evolves, its impact on our interaction with language will likely grow even further.

- Digital Assistants: Siri, Google Assistant, and Amazon Alexa are examples of AI-powered digital assistants that use natural language processing (NLP) to understand voice commands and respond human-likely. They can set reminders, provide weather updates, and answer queries.

- Machine Translation: Google Translate is a prominent example of machine translation. It uses AI to translate text, speech, images, or even real-time video from one language to another. DeepL is another advanced machine translation tool that uses AI.

- Chatbots: Businesses use AI-powered chatbots for customer service, sales, and marketing. These chatbots can understand and respond to customer queries, guiding them through troubleshooting steps or helping them make a purchase. Examples include IBM's Watson Assistant and the customer service chatbots used by many e-commerce companies.

- AI Writing and Content Generation: Tools like OpenAI's GPT-3 can generate human-like text, producing everything from news articles to poems. Companies also use AI for content creation in marketing, like writing product descriptions or generating social media posts.

- Email and Document Assistance: Tools like Grammarly and Microsoft Editor use AI to correct grammar and style, helping users improve their written communication. Google's Smart Compose feature in Gmail suggests completions to your writing sentences, another example of AI in language tasks.

- Speech Recognition and Transcription: Speech recognition technology, which converts spoken language into written text, is another application of AI. It is used in transcription services, voice-controlled assistants, and more. Examples include software like Dragon NaturallySpeaking and Google's voice typing feature.

- Sentiment Analysis: Many companies use AI to analyze customer feedback, social media comments, and product reviews to understand consumer sentiment. This can guide product development, marketing strategies, and customer service practices.

Chapter 32: AI and Food - Cooking with Algorithms

Artificial Intelligence (AI) is making its mark on the food industry in diverse and fascinating ways. From recipe development to supply chain optimization, AI reshapes how we produce, consume, and think about food.

The Use of AI in Recipe Development and Food Innovation

AI has brought a new dimension to recipe development and food innovation, leveraging vast data to create new flavor combinations, optimize nutritional content, and predict food trends.

- Recipe Creation: AI systems can analyze vast databases of recipes to identify common pairings and generate new recipes. For instance, IBM's "Chef Watson" uses cognitive computing to create novel recipes by combining ingredients in ways that would be hard for a human to conceive. This system considers not just flavor compatibility but also nutritional balance and novelty.

- Flavor Discovery and Optimization: AI can uncover new flavor profiles by analyzing chemical compounds in foods. For instance, a start-up called "Analytical Flavor Systems" uses machine learning to predict and design flavor profiles, helping food manufacturers develop new products that cater to consumer preferences.

- Nutritional Optimization: AI systems can also suggest modifications to recipes to make them healthier without compromising on taste. They can analyze a recipe's nutritional content and recommend substitutions or alterations to reduce calories, add protein, or increase fiber.

How AI is Transforming the Food Industry

Beyond recipe development, AI significantly influences various aspects of the food industry, from production to distribution to customer service.

- Agriculture and Food Production: In the agricultural sector, AI technologies like machine learning and computer vision optimize crop yield and reduce waste. Drones equipped with AI can monitor fields, identify issues like pests or diseases, and suggest treatment. AI can also predict crop yields based on weather patterns and other environmental factors.

- Supply Chain Management: AI can analyze historical data, real-time inputs, and future projections to optimize the food supply chain. It can predict demand, enabling better inventory management and reducing waste. AI can also track and optimize logistics, ensuring food is delivered most efficiently.
- Food Processing: AI-powered robots are increasingly used in food processing plants for sorting, packaging, and cooking tasks. These robots can work faster and more precisely than humans, increasing efficiency.
- Personalized Recommendations: Restaurants and food delivery services use AI to provide personalized customer recommendations based on their past orders, dietary preferences, and other factors. This enhances customer satisfaction and can also boost sales.

The Future of Food in an AI-Driven World

As AI continues to evolve, its impact on the food industry will likely grow, leading to exciting possibilities.

- Sustainable Production: AI could play a significant role in making food production more sustainable. It could optimize crop yields and reduce agricultural waste, contribute to the development of alternative proteins (like lab-grown meat), and improve the energy efficiency of food processing and distribution.
- Hyper-personalized Nutrition: In the future, we could see AI systems that provide hyper-personalized nutrition advice, tailoring recipes and

meal plans to an individual's specific health needs, taste preferences, and even genetic profile.

- Food Safety and Quality: AI could help improve food safety and quality. AI systems could monitor food for contamination or spoilage, predict shelf life, and detect food fraud.
- New Culinary Experiences: AI's ability to create novel recipes could lead to entirely new culinary experiences. We might see more restaurants and food manufacturers using AI to develop unique dishes and products that push the boundaries of taste and nutrition.

However, as with all technologies, adopting AI in the food industry will also present challenges. Data privacy, job displacement due to automation, and the risk of over-reliance on algorithms must be carefully managed. Nevertheless, AI is poised to dramatically change the food industry, promising significant benefits but requiring thoughtful stewardship.

Chapter 33: AI and Fashion - Designing with Data

Artificial Intelligence (AI) is causing a significant shift in the fashion industry, a realm traditionally governed by human creativity and intuition. The merger of fashion with data-driven AI transforms the fashion design and retail process and reshapes the entire industry's future. This chapter explores the role of AI in fashion design and retail, how it shapes the industry's future, and its broader implications.

The Role of AI in Fashion Design and Retail

AI's role in fashion design is remarkable, offering exciting potential for personalization, creativity, and efficiency. Designers can now utilize AI tools to analyze and learn from vast datasets comprising customer preferences, current trends, and historical fashion data. This can result in designs that cater more accurately to customer demand and emerging trends. For instance, companies like Stitch Fix are leveraging AI in their design process to create clothing based on user data, ensuring a more personalized and customer-centric approach.

AI also facilitates virtual modeling and digital fashion, visualizing garments on avatars or virtual models. This has the advantage of being more cost-effective and versatile, allowing for rapid prototyping and experimentation. In addition, AI also promotes sustainable practices by reducing the need for physical samples, thereby reducing waste.

In retail, AI is primarily deployed to enhance the customer experience, increase operational efficiency, and boost sales. AI-powered chatbots, for example, can provide personalized fashion advice, customer service, and product recommendations. In addition, the predictive abilities of AI can be harnessed for inventory management, optimizing stock levels based on anticipated demand to minimize overstocking and understocking. Furthermore, AI can be used for dynamic pricing, adjusting prices in real time based on factors like demand, season, and trends.

How AI is Shaping the Future of the Fashion Industry

The fusion of AI and fashion has initiated a transformative journey, bringing futuristic concepts into the present. This evolution is shaping the future of the fashion industry in several ways.

AI-powered predictive analytics is set to redefine trend forecasting, making it more precise and timely. By analyzing data from diverse sources like social media, online search behavior, and e-commerce platforms, AI can spot emerging fashion trends earlier and more accurately than traditional methods.

Virtual and augmented reality, powered by AI, are set to become more mainstream. For example, virtual fashion shows and AR fitting rooms could provide a novel, immersive shopping experience that bridges the gap between online and offline retail.

Sustainability, a critical concern in the fashion industry, can also be addressed through AI. AI can optimize manufacturing processes, supply chains, and inventory management, reducing waste and promoting sustainable practices.

AI is also making strides in the realm of personalized fashion. For example, AI algorithms can create custom designs tailored to individual tastes, body shapes, and needs. This level of personalization, once a luxury, could become commonplace.

The Implications of AI in Fashion

The integration of AI in fashion carries significant implications, presenting a mix of opportunities and challenges.

On the positive side, AI can democratize fashion, making personalized, high-quality designs accessible to a broader audience. It also has the potential to make the fashion industry more sustainable by optimizing production and reducing waste. From an economic perspective, integrating AI can increase efficiency and profitability in the fashion industry, from design and manufacturing to retail and customer service. It can also open new job opportunities like data analysis, machine learning, and user experience design.

However, the rise of AI in fashion also poses potential challenges. Automating certain tasks could lead to job displacement in design, production, and retail areas. There are also concerns about data privacy, as personalized fashion relies heavily on collecting and analyzing personal data. Furthermore, while AI can simulate human creativity to a certain extent, it cannot fully replicate the human touch, intuition, and emotional intelligence inherent in fashion design. AI is causing a transformative shift in the fashion industry, offering exciting opportunities for creativity, personalization, and efficiency. However, its rise also necessitates careful consideration of issues like job displacement, data privacy, and the preservation of human creativity. As we look to the future, the challenge lies in leveraging AI's potential in a way that complements rather than replaces human creativity and ingenuity and in doing so responsibly and ethically.

Chapter 34: AI and Archaeology - Unearthing the Past with Algorithms

In the interdisciplinary field of archaeology, which merges human history with scientific techniques, artificial intelligence (AI) is gradually transforming traditional methods of analysis, preservation, and interpretation of the past. This chapter explores how AI is employed in archaeological analysis and preservation, reshaping our understanding of history and its potential future in archaeology.

The Use of AI in Archaeological Analysis and Preservation

Artificial intelligence, with its pattern-recognition abilities and data analysis capabilities, is revolutionizing how archaeologists analyze and preserve artifacts, monuments, and archaeological sites.

- Automated Artifact Analysis: AI, particularly machine learning, is being used to analyze archaeological artifacts, helping to classify them based on their shape, size, material, and other features. Computer vision, a subfield of AI, can identify and classify images of artifacts more quickly and consistently than humans can, thereby speeding up the analysis process.

- Remote Sensing and Site Detection: AI algorithms are also used to analyze data from remote sensing technologies like LiDAR and satellite imagery. They can identify potential archaeological sites by detecting patterns and anomalies indicative of human activity, even under dense vegetation or in inaccessible areas.

- Digital Preservation: AI is used to digitally preserve heritage sites, creating detailed 3D models from photographs and scans. This allows for virtual tours of these sites and helps to preserve their memory in case of destruction or degradation.

How AI is Changing the Way We Understand History

AI fundamentally changes how we understand history by improving our ability to analyze and interpret archaeological data.

- Enhanced Accuracy and Consistency: With the ability to process large amounts of data quickly and consistently, AI can help minimize human error and bias in archaeological analysis. This can lead to more accurate and reliable interpretations of the past.

- Broader Patterns and Connections: AI's ability to analyze large datasets can reveal broader patterns and connections that might be missed with traditional analysis methods. For example, it could help identify cultural connections between different regions based on similarities in artifacts or architectural styles.

- Democratization of History: By making archaeological analysis more efficient, AI could help make the study of history more accessible. AI tools could allow smaller teams or even amateur archaeologists to carry out sophisticated analyses that were previously possible only for large research institutions.

The Future of Archaeology in an AI-Driven World

As AI continues to evolve, its impact on archaeology will likely grow. Here are some ways AI could shape the future of archaeology:

- Predictive Modeling: AI could create predictive models that suggest where important archaeological sites or artifacts might be found. This could help guide excavation efforts and conserve resources.

- Deep Learning in Archaeology: Advanced AI techniques like deep learning could be used to analyze complex archaeological data, such as deciphering ancient texts or identifying subtle stylistic changes in artifacts over time.

- Augmented Reality (AR) and Virtual Reality (VR): AI could enhance AR and VR applications in archaeology, providing immersive experiences that help researchers and the public better understand and appreciate archaeological sites.

However, as with all fields impacted by AI, these advancements come with challenges. These include ethical considerations regarding data privacy and the potential reduction of hands-on field experience for archaeologists. Furthermore, while AI can assist with many tasks, it is not a replacement for human expertise and judgment. AI should be seen as a tool that augments rather than replaces the skills of archaeologists. Nevertheless, AI is reshaping archaeology profoundly, aiding in analyzing and preserving our shared heritage and changing how we understand history. As we look to the future, the challenge lies in leveraging the potential of AI while also addressing its ethical and practical challenges. It will be an exciting journey, merging the wisdom of the past with the technology of the future.

Chapter 35: AI and Music - The Symphony of Algorithms

Artificial Intelligence (AI) is gradually orchestrating a new era in the music industry, expanding its influence from composition and production to the broader music industry. This chapter explores the role of AI in music composition and production, the implications of AI in the music industry, and the future of music in an AI-driven world.

The Role of AI in Music Composition and Production

AI's role in music composition is intriguing, as it challenges the traditional notion that musical creativity is an exclusively human trait. Over recent years, AI technologies have been developed that can compose music in various styles, from classical symphonies to catchy pop tunes. AI music composition systems like OpenAI's MuseNet use deep learning algorithms to generate music. First, they are trained on large datasets containing diverse musical styles, from which they learn musical patterns and structures. Then, once trained, these systems can generate new compositions that reflect their learned styles.

AI can also aid in the process of music production. AI-powered software can assist with tasks like mixing and mastering, which require technical skills and are time-consuming. In addition, these tools can automatically adjust levels, EQ, and other parameters to achieve a balanced mix, significantly speeding up the production process.

The Implications of AI in the Music Industry

Integrating AI in the music industry has several far-reaching implications, presenting opportunities and challenges.

On the one hand, AI can democratize music creation and production, making it accessible to individuals without formal music training or technical production skills. This could lead to a surge of creativity and diversity in the music scene as more people gain the ability to express themselves through music.

AI also can potentially transform the business side of the music industry. For example, AI algorithms can predict music trends, giving artists and record labels valuable insights into what songs will likely be popular. Furthermore, AI can enhance music recommendation systems, making them more accurate and personalized.

However, the rise of AI in music also poses potential challenges. One is the question of copyright and ownership of music created by AI. Current copyright laws are not equipped to handle works created by AI, leading to legal grey areas. There are also concerns about the impact of AI on jobs in the music industry. While AI can certainly assist with tasks like composition and production, it could potentially replace human roles in these areas.

The Future of Music in an AI-Driven World

As AI advances, its impact on music will likely grow. Here are some possible future directions:

- Collaboration between AI and Humans: AI could become a standard tool for musicians, much like a digital instrument, helping them to express their ideas and improve their work. Musicians might work in tandem with AI, using it to generate ideas and refine their compositions.
- Personalized Music: AI could create personalized music tailored to individual listeners' tastes. For example, it could generate custom soundtracks to accompany a workout or meditation session.
- AI Performances: We might see more performances by AI, either in virtual concerts or collaborations with human musicians.

Despite these exciting possibilities, the future of music in an AI-driven world also necessitates careful consideration of its challenges, including ethical, legal, and societal issues. It is important to balance leveraging AI's potential and preserving the uniquely human elements of music. AI is causing a transformative shift in the music industry, bringing new possibilities for creativity, accessibility, and business insights. However, this shift also brings complex challenges that require thoughtful discussion and careful navigation. As we embrace this new era of AI in music and the symphony of algorithms, the challenge lies in ensuring that this powerful tool enhances rather than replaces human creativity and expression.

Chapter 36: AI and Religion - Faith in Algorithms

Artificial Intelligence (AI) is no longer a stranger to any field or discipline, and religion is no exception. The intersection of AI and religion opens up intriguing questions about the role of technology in religious practices, theological reflections, and the ethical and societal implications it could bring. This chapter explores these aspects and deliberates on the potential future of religion in an AI-driven world.

The Role of AI in Religious Practices and Theological Reflections

AI is gradually finding its place within religious practices and theological reflections. Although not replacing the depth of human spiritual experiences, AI can augment and enhance certain aspects of religious practices.

- AI in Liturgical Practices: AI can automate certain religious rituals or services. For instance, there have been examples of Buddhist temples using robot priests to chant sutras and Christian churches employing AI to translate biblical texts.
- AI in Theological Reflections: AI's ability to analyze large amounts of data could be used to offer new insights into religious texts. Using natural language processing (NLP), AI could examine patterns, themes, and connections across religious literature.
- AI and Religious Engagement: AI chatbots, equipped with knowledge about religious texts and principles, can serve as virtual religious advisors, providing guidance or answering questions about religious teachings.

The Ethical and Societal Implications of AI in Religion

The application of AI in religion brings about significant ethical and societal implications.

- Privacy Concerns: As with any field where AI is employed, there are concerns about data privacy. Sensitive information disclosed during a virtual religious advisory session could be misused if proper data protection measures are not in place.
- The AI 'God' Dilemma: The advancement of AI prompts theological questions about the nature of divinity. Could an omnipotent, omniscient AI be considered a form of 'god'? This sparked debates about idolatry, creation, and the nature of divine intelligence.

- The authenticity of Experience: There is an ongoing debate about whether an AI can truly replicate the depth and nuance of a religious leader's guidance or a communal worship experience.

The Future of Religion in an AI-driven World

The advent of AI is likely to further to mold the landscape of religion in intriguing ways:

- Enhanced Religious Education: Future AI applications could personalize religious education based on a person's learning style and pace, improving the accessibility and comprehension of religious teachings.
- Interfaith Understanding: AI's ability to analyze and cross-reference religious texts from different traditions could promote greater interfaith understanding and dialogue.
- Virtual Reality and Spirituality: With virtual reality, AI could create immersive spiritual experiences, such as virtual pilgrimages or meditative environments.

Despite these potential advancements, it is crucial to approach the integration of AI into religion with caution, sensitivity, and respect for religious traditions and values. As AI evolves, religious communities, theologians, and technologists must engage in ongoing dialogue to navigate this complex intersection responsibly. AI brings intriguing possibilities to religious practices and theological reflections, prompting us to re-evaluate the interaction between faith and technology. The future of religion in an AI-driven world is a vast and unchartered landscape. It calls for careful deliberation on how AI can best serve religious communities, foster spiritual growth, and respect the sanctity of religious traditions and experiences. The challenge lies in how we harmonize this symphony of faith and algorithms.

Chapter 37: AI and Gaming - Playing with Algorithms

Artificial Intelligence (AI) has deeply intertwined itself with the gaming industry, playing a pivotal role in revolutionizing game design, enhancing player interactions, and creating unprecedented changes in the gaming landscape. This section explores the role of AI in game design and player interactions, the impact AI is making on the gaming industry, and the potential future of gaming in an AI-driven world.

The Role of AI in Game Design and Player Interactions

AI's presence in game design is longstanding, dating back to early computer games where AI was used to create basic opponent behavior. However, recent advancements in AI technology have far exceeded these rudimentary applications, making it an integral part of game design and player interactions.

- Procedural Content Generation: AI can dynamically create vast, intricate game environments rather than requiring designers to craft each element by hand. Games like "No Man's Sky" use procedural generation to create a virtually infinite universe for players to explore.
- AI-driven Non-Player Characters (NPCs): AI helps develop intelligent NPCs that can learn and adapt to players' actions, offering a more realistic and challenging gaming experience. AI algorithms can learn from players' behaviors to anticipate their moves and respond more intelligently.
- Personalization: AI can analyze player behavior to personalize game experiences, adjust difficulty levels, suggest in-game items, or modify storylines based on the player's actions and preferences.

How AI is Changing the Landscape of the Gaming Industry

The influx of AI in the gaming industry has brought significant shifts and opportunities.

- Evolving Game Design: AI in game design leads to more complex, immersive, and personalized games. It allows developers to create dynamic worlds that react and evolve based on player behavior, leading to a more immersive gaming experience.
- Player Analytics and Monetization: AI-driven analytics can offer insights into player behavior, preferences, and spending habits, which can be used

to enhance player retention and optimize monetization strategies.

- Cheating Detection: AI can help detect and prevent cheating by recognizing irregular patterns in player behavior that suggest cheating or exploitation of game mechanics.

The Future of Gaming in an AI-driven World

As AI technology continues to advance, it is poised to redefine the future of gaming by:

- Advancements in Virtual and Augmented Reality: VR and AR games could become more immersive and interactive with AI. AI could interpret players' physical movements more accurately, allow game environments to adapt in real-time, and create more intelligent and lifelike NPCs.
- Emotionally Responsive Gaming: Future games might use AI to recognize players' emotions through facial expressions, voice tone, or physiological signals and adjust the game accordingly.
- Co-Creation of Games: AI could eventually become a collaborative partner in the game development process, helping designers to brainstorm ideas, automate routine tasks, and even generate elements of the game on its own.

Despite the promise AI holds for the gaming industry, it also presents challenges that must be addressed, including ethical considerations around data privacy, the potential for AI-generated content to infringe on intellectual property rights, and the risk of AI being used to cheat or disrupt games. Nevertheless, AI's integration into gaming is reshaping the industry, ushering in a new era of interactive entertainment.

As we step into the future of gaming in an AI-driven world, the challenge lies in harnessing the potential of AI while also navigating its challenges responsibly. The game of the future is not just about playing with algorithms but also about understanding and managing their impact on the gaming experience and the industry.

Chapter 38: AI and Insurance - Predicting the Future

With its vast amounts of data and the inherent need for foresight, the insurance industry is ripe for disruption by AI. This section discusses the influence of AI on risk assessment and policy pricing and the transformation AI is driving in the insurance industry, and the prospective future of insurance in an AI-driven world.

The Use of AI in Risk Assessment and Policy Pricing

Risk assessment and policy pricing form the bedrock of insurance, and AI has brought about innovative ways to execute several critical functions by:

- Automated Underwriting: AI models can analyze various data points from different sources in real time to assess risk, improving the speed and accuracy of underwriting. Automated underwriting helps insurers streamline their operations and improve their risk management.
- Dynamic Pricing Models: AI can create dynamic pricing models that adjust policy prices based on real-time data. For instance, AI can monitor driving behavior in real-time to adjust car insurance premiums, a model known as usage-based insurance.
- Fraud Detection: AI systems can detect anomalies in claim patterns that might indicate fraudulent activity, thus protecting insurers from potential losses.

How AI is Transforming the Insurance Industry

AI's impact extends across the insurance value chain, causing a seismic shift in the industry.

- Customer Service: AI-powered chatbots and virtual assistants are improving customer interactions by providing round-the-clock service and instant responses to inquiries.
- Claims Processing: AI can automate claims processing, making it faster and more efficient. Algorithms can assess damage in photos, review policy details, and process payments, often in a fraction of the time it would take a human.
- Predictive Analytics: AI can analyze vast datasets to predict future trends and risks, helping insurers anticipate market shifts and adjust their strategies proactively.

The Future of Insurance in an AI-driven World

As AI continues to evolve, it promises to revolutionize the insurance industry further by:

- Personalized Policies: AI could enable hyper-personalization of insurance policies, tailoring coverage and pricing to individual needs and risk profiles.
- Preventive Insurance: AI could shift the industry from a compensation model to prevention by predicting risks. Insurers might provide customers with AI-driven advice or tools to help them mitigate risks before they occur.
- Blockchain and AI: Combining AI and blockchain could create a transparent, efficient, secure insurance industry. Blockchain could provide a secure platform for sharing data, while AI could analyze that data to make accurate risk assessments and automate processes.

Despite the potential benefits, incorporating AI into insurance also brings challenges. These include data privacy issues, AI algorithms' transparency, and the potential displacement of human jobs. Insurers must navigate these issues carefully to realize the full benefits of AI. Moreover, AI is not just predicting the future of insurance—it is actively creating it. The insurance industry, traditionally considered slow to innovate, is now at the forefront of AI adoption. As we look to an AI-driven future, it is clear that the insurance industry stands to gain from AI's ability to predict risks, streamline operations, and enhance customer service. Nevertheless, with these opportunities come challenges requiring careful consideration, planning, and oversight. The future of insurance in an AI-driven world has immense potential, underscored by the need for responsible AI use.

Chapter 39: AI and the Human Body - Augmenting our Capabilities

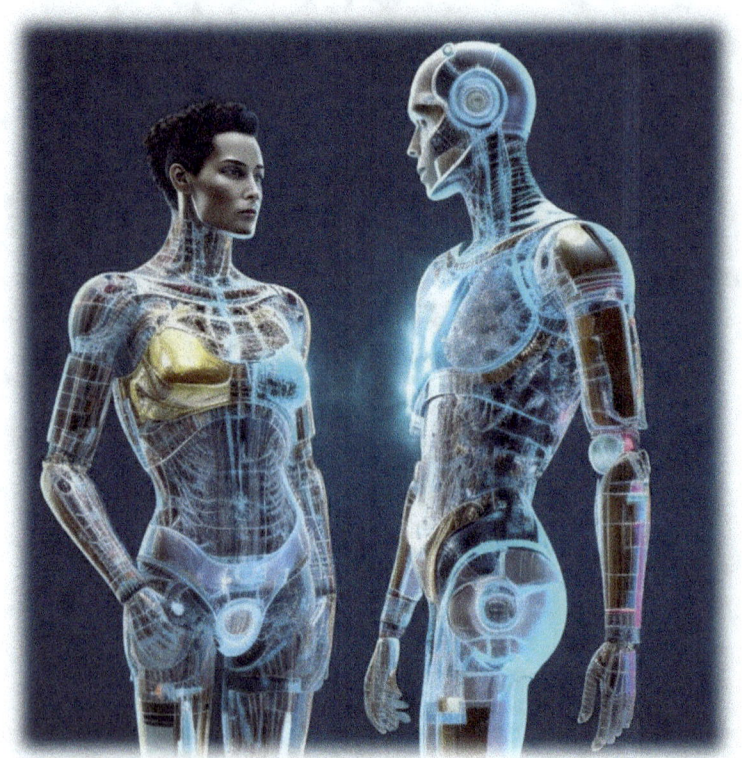

Artificial Intelligence (AI) has begun to permeate human physiology, with potential applications ranging from personal health tracking to advanced body augmentation. In this section, I discuss the role of AI in these areas, the ethical and societal implications it brings, and the potential future of the human body in an AI-driven world.

The Role of AI in Personal Health Tracking and Body Augmentation

AI has a significant role in tracking health parameters and augmenting physical capabilities, with applications growing more sophisticated yearly.

- Personal Health Tracking: Wearable devices, such as smartwatches and fitness trackers, use AI to monitor health data like heart rate, sleep patterns, and physical activity. These devices can provide personalized insights and recommendations, helping individuals to maintain and improve their health.
- AI-Enabled Prosthetics: Advanced AI algorithms create prosthetic limbs that respond to neural signals, allowing for more natural and intuitive movement. For example, AI-powered bionic hands can perform complex tasks by interpreting muscular signals from the wearer.
- Predictive Health: AI systems can analyze health data to predict potential medical issues, enabling preventative care. For instance, AI algorithms can analyze heart rate variability data to predict potential cardiovascular problems.
- The Ethical and Societal Implications of AI in Body Augmentation
- As AI interfaces more deeply with the human body, it raises several ethical and societal concerns that must be carefully considered:
- Privacy and Data Security: The collection and analysis of personal health data by AI systems raise concerns about data privacy and security. The risk of mishandling or misusing sensitive health data could seriously affect individuals.

- Accessibility and Equity: Advanced AI-driven body augmentations are often costly, raising concerns about who has access to these technologies. There is a risk of exacerbating societal inequities if only those who can afford these technologies benefit from them.
- Human Identity and Dignity: The augmentation of human capabilities through AI may also raise existential questions about what it means to be human. Society and psychological implications may exist as people adapt to these technologies and navigate their enhanced abilities.

The Future of the Human Body in an AI-driven World

Looking forward, the integration of AI with the human body holds significant promise but also raises some theoretical questions:

- Superhuman Abilities: As AI technologies advance, they could give rise to "superhuman" abilities. For example, AI-powered exoskeletons could enable individuals to lift heavy weights or run at high speeds.
- Brain-Computer Interfaces: Research is underway to develop AI-powered brain-computer interfaces that could enable direct communication between the human brain and digital devices. This could transform how we interact with technology, communicate, and think.
- Personalized Healthcare: AI could lead to a future where healthcare is highly personalized, with AI systems monitoring individual health data in real time and providing customized advice and treatments.

AI and the human body are ushering in a new era of potential human capability with profound implications for society and individuals. However, as we grapple with these technologies' ethical and societal challenges, we must ensure they are used responsibly and equitably. The future of the human body in an AI-driven world is a fascinating frontier, promising a blend of opportunities, challenges, and profound questions about the very nature of human existence.

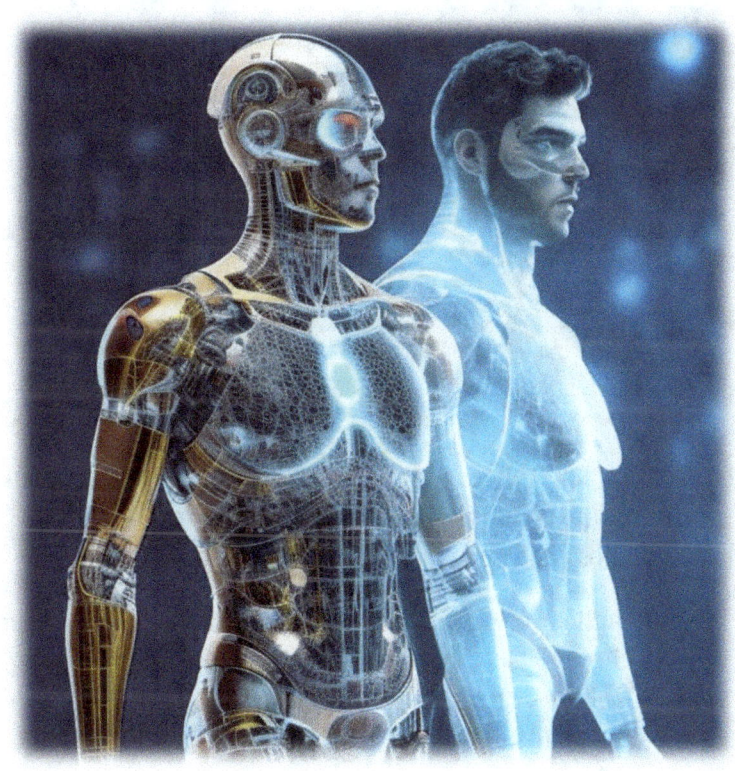

Hospitals and AI

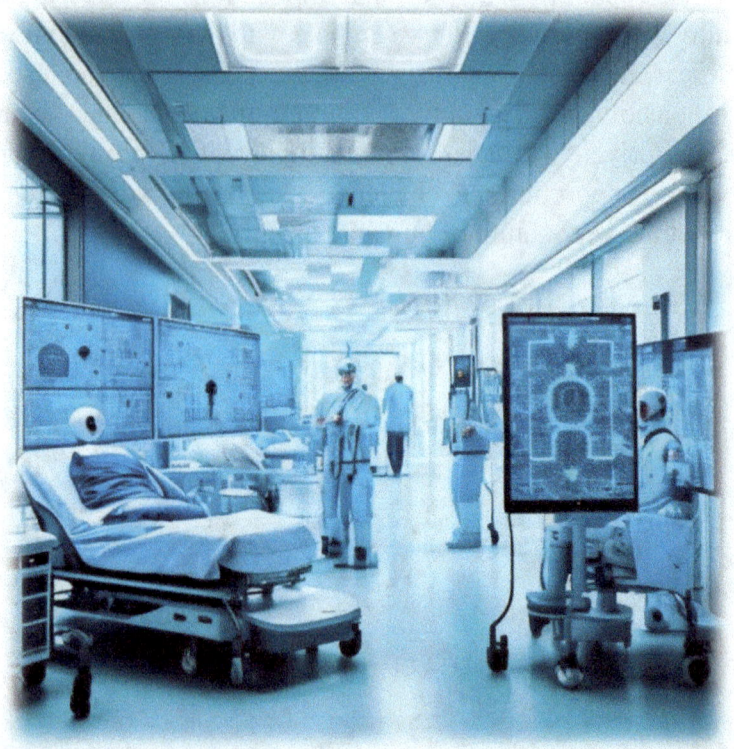

Artificial Intelligence (AI) is being adopted in hospitals worldwide, revolutionizing healthcare delivery. Here are a few ways hospitals are starting to use AI:

- Diagnostic Imaging: AI algorithms can assist radiologists in interpreting medical imaging. Machine learning models can identify patterns and abnormalities in MRIs, CT scans, and X-rays that might be missed by the human eye, thus improving the accuracy of diagnoses.
- Predictive Analytics: Hospitals use AI algorithms to predict patient outcomes based on data such as

medical history, vital signs, and diagnostic results. This allows for better risk assessment, helping doctors to intervene earlier when complications are predicted.

- Virtual Health Assistants: AI is also used as chatbots and virtual health assistants, providing patients with immediate responses to their queries, helping schedule appointments, and offering basic healthcare and medication advice.
- Remote Monitoring and Telemedicine: AI-enabled wearable devices monitor patients' health in real-time, alerting healthcare providers to any significant changes. This is particularly useful for patients with chronic diabetes or heart disease.
- Robotic Surgery: Robots, guided by AI and human surgeons, can perform complex procedures with high precision. These surgeries can be less invasive and can lead to quicker recovery times.
- Automated Administrative Tasks: AI can automate administrative tasks like billing, scheduling, and maintaining patient records. This reduces the workload on administrative staff and allows for more efficient hospital operations.
- Drug Discovery: AI is used to analyze vast databases of existing medicines, predict their potential new uses, and design new drugs based on understanding diseases at the molecular level.
- Precision Medicine: AI algorithms can analyze a patient's genetic information and lifestyle factors to provide personalized treatment plans. This is a shift away from a "one-size-fits-all" approach to healthcare.

While these applications present immense opportunities, they also raise challenges, including data privacy concerns, extensive testing and validation, and the need for clinicians to develop new skills and understand these technologies' limitations and functioning. It is crucial to address these challenges to harness the full potential of AI in the hospital setting.

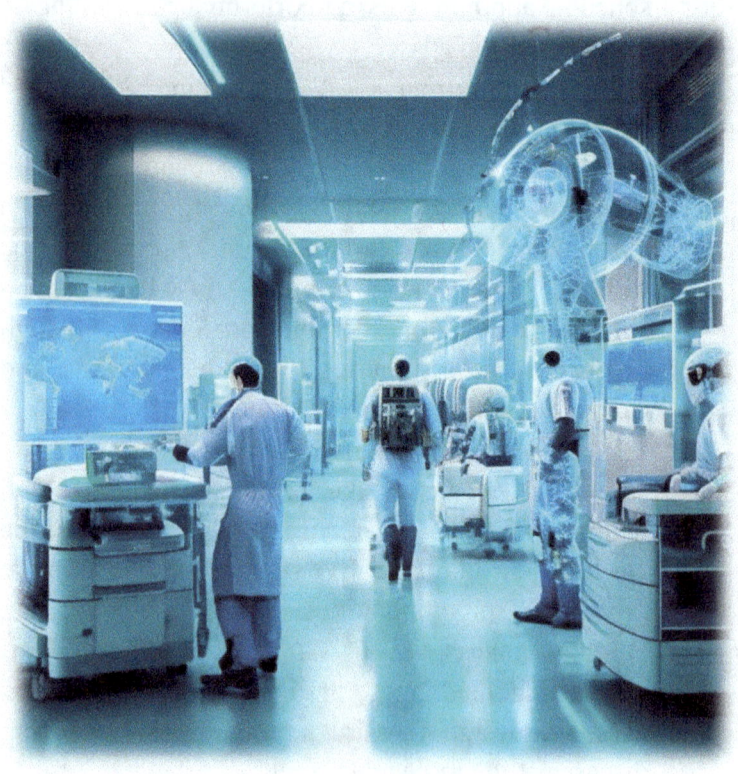

Chapter 40: AI and the Animal Kingdom - Understanding our Fellow Inhabitants

Integrating Artificial Intelligence (AI) into zoology and conservation biology is ushering in a new age of understanding and interaction with the animal kingdom. The application of AI in animal behavior studies and conservation, its implications for our comprehension of animal life, and the prospective future of animal studies in an AI-driven world.

The Use of AI in Animal Behavior Studies and Conservation Efforts

AI has a remarkable role in studying animal behavior and promoting conservation efforts, with increasingly diverse and sophisticated applications.

- Behavioral Analysis: With AI and machine learning techniques, scientists can analyze animal behavior non-invasive and highly detailedly. These technologies can process and interpret vast amounts of data collected from video surveillance or tagging devices, providing insights into behavioral patterns and social structures.

- Species Identification and Population Tracking: AI tools can identify species and individuals within a species by learning distinctive characteristics from images, videos, or audio recordings. This aids researchers in tracking population numbers and movements, crucial elements in conservation efforts.

- Habitat Evaluation: AI algorithms can analyze satellite imagery and other data sources to assess changes in animal habitats over time. These evaluations can highlight threats like deforestation or climate change, informing conservation strategies.

The Implications of AI in Our Understanding of the Animal Kingdom

The utilization of AI in animal studies enriches our understanding of the animal kingdom in a multitude of ways:

- Enhanced Knowledge: AI allows for a more detailed and systematic study of animal behavior and biology, enabling us to uncover complexities we might otherwise miss.

- Conservation Success: AI-driven conservation efforts can better preserve biodiversity, leading to a more accurate understanding of the interconnectedness of the natural world.
- Inter-Species Communication: Some research is even looking into using AI to interpret animal sounds, gestures, and movements, potentially paving the way for more direct interspecies communication.

The Future of Animal Studies in an AI-driven World

The integration of AI with animal studies heralds a future of intriguing possibilities.

- Automated Conservation: As AI technologies improve, we may see automated systems that monitor and protect wildlife, respond to threats, and restore damaged habitats.
- AI-Driven Animal Research: Advanced AI might help us understand animal cognition and emotions deeper, possibly redefining our relationships with animals.
- Preventive Measures: By predicting changes and threats to animal habitats, AI can help us take preventative measures, enabling proactive rather than reactive conservation efforts.

However, the fusion of AI and animal studies also brings challenges. Privacy and ethical issues concerning the extensive monitoring of animals must be addressed. Furthermore, as AI systems require large amounts of data, ensuring the collection methods are non-invasive and non-harmful to animals is paramount. The intersection of AI and animal studies is an emerging frontier, offering exciting opportunities and novel challenges. It allows us to deepen our understanding of the animal kingdom and refine our conservation efforts, ensuring the preservation of biodiversity. As we move into an AI-driven future, the use of AI in animal studies underscores the necessity of maintaining ethical and respectful interactions with our fellow inhabitants. The future of animal studies in an AI-driven world promises a new paradigm of understanding and cohabitation, marrying technological innovation with biological marvel.

tourism, the ABCs of AI form the underlying bedrock of its diverse applications.

Final Thoughts on the Transformative Potential of AI and Its Implications for the Future of Our World

There is little doubt that AI holds transformative potential. It catalyzes unprecedented change across sectors, revolutionizing how we work, communicate, create, and even think. However, with this potential comes responsibility.

While AI can be a powerful tool for progress, it is not a panacea. It has its limitations and pitfalls; we must be conscious of them as we move forward. We need to ensure that the development and deployment of AI are guided by a robust ethical framework that considers questions of fairness, transparency, privacy, and accountability.

Moreover, bridging the digital divide and ensuring equal access to its benefits is essential as AI advances. Technology should be a democratizing force, not one that exacerbates inequalities.

Existential Questions and Concerns Raised by AI

AI also provokes profound existential questions and concerns. For example, what does being human mean as machines become more intelligent and capable? What value do we place on uniquely human qualities like empathy, creativity, and moral judgment?

Furthermore, as we delegate more decisions to AI, how do we ensure it aligns with our values and interests? Finally, and perhaps most significantly, how do we prepare for a future where AI has the potential to exceed human intelligence?

These questions do not have easy answers, and addressing them requires a collective, multidisciplinary effort. Nevertheless, it is crucial that we engage in these discussions now, as the choices we make will shape the trajectory of AI and, in turn, the future of our world. Our journey through the world of AI has been a tale of awe-inspiring possibilities, sobering realities, and profound questions. As we stand on the precipice of an AI-driven era, we have the opportunity and responsibility to shape a future that harnesses the power of AI for the benefit of all. As we continue to explore and understand this fascinating technology, let us do so with a spirit of curiosity, caution, and an unwavering commitment to our shared human values.

Conclusion: Living with AI - Adapting to a New Normal

We stand on the cusp of a new age that promises to be as transformative and disruptive as the Industrial Revolution. The revolution this time, however, is not driven by steam engines but by artificial intelligence. As we navigate this brave new world, the task that lies before us is twofold: to embrace this AI Revolution and adapt to the 'new normal' it ushers in. In this closing discussion, I will explore these themes, delving into the importance of understanding and engaging with AI, the roles of different stakeholders, and how we can adapt to an increasingly AI-driven world.

Embracing the AI Revolution

The AI Revolution is here, transforming every facet of our lives. AI is changing the game's rules from how we shop and communicate to how we work, learn, and entertain ourselves. Embracing this revolution means recognizing AI's transformative potential and being open to the changes it brings. However, it also means understanding its limitations and ethical implications. As we stand at the precipice of this technological leap, embracing AI should be a thoughtful and informed decision rather than a blind leap of faith.

The Importance of Understanding and Engaging with AI

Understanding AI is crucial, not just for technologists but for everyone. As AI becomes increasingly integrated into our daily lives, it is essential to understand how it works, its benefits, and its risks. This understanding empowers us to use AI effectively, to make informed decisions about its use, and to participate in discussions about its regulation and control.

Engaging with AI is equally critical. We are not passive recipients of the AI Revolution but active participants. Our interactions with AI – from the data we generate to the tools we use – shape its development. Moreover, our voices and perspectives can influence the policies and regulations that govern AI.

The Role of Individuals, Governments, and Organizations in Shaping AI's Future

Individuals, governments, and organizations are pivotal in shaping AI's future. We must stay informed about AI, use it responsibly, and advocate for ethical AI practices.

Governments must create robust regulatory frameworks that promote AI innovation while protecting societal interests. Furthermore, organizations, whether they are tech companies developing AI or businesses using AI, must prioritize transparency, fairness, and respect for privacy.

Reflecting on the Pervasive Impact of AI in Every Facet of Life

AI's impact is pervasive, touching every facet of life. It shapes our economies, alters our workplaces, and changes our social fabric. It is revolutionizing sectors as diverse as healthcare, education, retail, and entertainment. However, it also raises questions about privacy, job displacement, and inequality. Reflecting on this impact helps us appreciate the magnitude of the AI Revolution and the importance of navigating it wisely.

How to Adapt to a World Increasingly Driven by AI

Adapting to an AI-driven world requires a blend of skills and attitudes. Lifelong learning is crucial, as AI changes the skillsets required in the workplace. Digital literacy, including a basic understanding of AI, is increasingly important. Adaptability, creativity, and critical thinking – skills AI has yet to master – are also valuable. Furthermore, an open yet critical mindset will allow us to embrace AI without ignoring its risks and implications.

A Call to Action for Responsible AI Use and Advocacy

As I conclude, we must make a call to action for responsible AI use and advocacy. Let us use AI in ways that respect human rights and dignity, promote fairness and inclusivity, and consider societal and environmental impacts. Let us advocate for ethical, transparent, and accountable AI.

Furthermore, let us ensure that the AI Revolution is a revolution for all, bringing benefits and opportunities to every corner of the globe.

Final Thoughts on the Journey of AI and Its Impact on Society

In closing, the journey of AI is a journey we are all on together. It is a journey that promises to be exciting, transformative, challenging, and fraught with ethical dilemmas. However, as we move forward, let us remember that AI is not an end but a tool. A tool that, in our hands, has the power to shape a future that reflects our shared values and aspirations.

Glossary: Understanding AI Jargon

AI is replete with jargon and terms that can feel overwhelming to those new to the field. However, a basic understanding of these terms can greatly facilitate comprehension of AI discussions. This glossary aims to provide definitions of some key AI terms and phrases.

- *Artificial Intelligence (AI):* Broadly, AI refers to the capability of a machine to imitate intelligent human behavior. It is a multidisciplinary field that includes machine learning, natural language processing, robotics, and more.
- *Machine Learning (ML):* This is a subset of AI where machines are given access to data and use it to learn for themselves. It is the method by which our digital assistants learn our daily routines and how self-driving cars learn to make turns.
- *Deep Learning (DL):* A further subset of machine learning, deep learning algorithms attempt to model high-level abstractions in data using model architectures composed of multiple nonlinear transformations.
- *Neural Networks:* These are a set of algorithms modeled after the human brain, designed to recognize patterns. They interpret sensory data through machine perception, labeling, or clustering raw input.
- *Natural Language Processing (NLP):* This branch of AI helps computers understand, interpret, and utilize human language. NLP allows for human-computer interaction, content summarization, and sentiment analysis, among other applications.

- **Supervised Learning:** This is a type of machine learning where an AI is trained using a labeled dataset, where the "correct" answers are provided. The goal of supervised learning is to learn a function that, given a sample of data and desired outputs, best approximates the relationship between input and output observable in the data.
- **Unsupervised Learning:** This is another type of machine learning where AI is given unlabeled data and must find patterns and relationships within the data itself.
- **Reinforcement Learning:** This is a type of machine learning where an agent learns to behave in an environment by performing certain actions and observing the results.
- **Artificial General Intelligence (AGI):** This refers to artificial intelligence as smart as a human in all aspects of cognitive functioning, including problem-solving, understanding emotions and language, and creativity.
- **Predictive Analytics:** This uses data, statistical algorithms, and machine learning techniques to identify the likelihood of future outcomes based on historical data. It is all about providing the best assessment of what will happen.
- **Chatbots**: AI software designed to interact with humans in their natural languages. These AI usually converse via auditory or textual means and are commonly used for customer service or information acquisition.
- **Robotics Process Automation (RPA):** This refers to using AI or bots to automate highly repetitive tasks usually performed by humans.

- ***Computer Vision:*** This field involves training machines to interpret and understand the visual world. Computers can accurately identify and classify objects—and then react to what they "see."
- ***Data Mining:*** This is discovering patterns in large data sets involving methods at the intersection of machine learning, statistics, and database systems.

Understanding these terms will provide a solid foundation for anyone interested in delving deeper into the AI landscape. AI is a dynamic and evolving field; this glossary is not exhaustive. As you continue to explore AI, you will undoubtedly encounter new terms and concepts, adding to the richness and excitement of your AI journey.

Epilogue: The Journey from Dawn to Adaptation - An AI Odyssey

As we reach the end of our AI odyssey, we are left in awe of the expansive landscape of artificial intelligence and its profound and far-reaching implications. From the dawn of the AI concept to the ubiquitous integration of AI systems in our daily lives, understanding AI has exercised intellectual curiosity and profound revelation. Reflecting on this journey, one cannot help but appreciate the immense transformative potential of AI and the existential questions it raises.

Introduction: The Dawn of Artificial Intelligence

I began our journey by defining AI and tracing its birth from Turing's machine to the first AI programs. This foundational understanding laid the groundwork for exploring AI's deeper, more complex aspects.

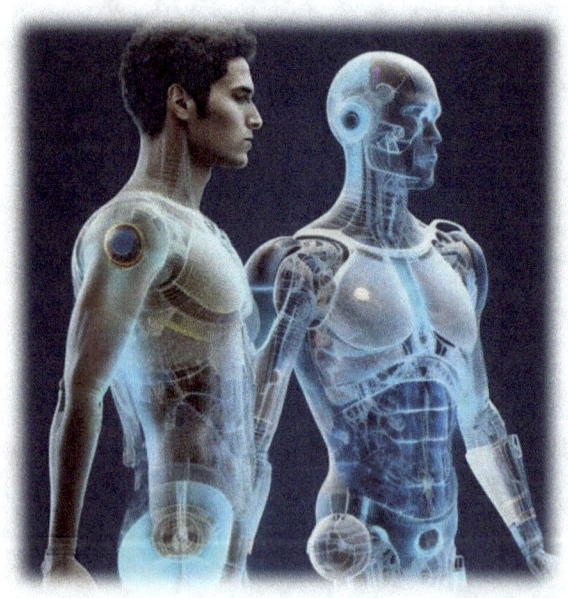

Chapter 1: The Evolution of AI - A Journey from Turing to Today

This chapter studied the major milestones in AI development, witnessing its influence on society and industries. I also unpacked the Turing test, a seminal concept in the AI narrative that gauges a machine's ability to exhibit intelligent behavior indistinguishable from a human's.

Chapter 2: The Mechanics of AI - Simplified

With a grasp on the history of AI, I dove into its basic principles - machine learning and deep learning - which power its cognitive abilities. We now understand how data, algorithms, and computation act as the building blocks of AI and have learned about different types of AI - Narrow AI, General AI, and Super intelligent AI.

Chapter 3: AI in Today's World - Applications and Implications

As AI became less of an abstract concept, I turned our attention to its real-world applications, ranging from everyday life, like smartphones and smart homes, to businesses in healthcare, finance, and beyond. Finally, we examined notable real-world examples of AI in action, such as Microsoft's Copilot.

Chapter 4 - 26: The Multifaceted Implications of AI

In the subsequent chapters, we explored the various facets of AI's integration into our lives. I discussed AI's transformative influence and ethical conundrums from governance, social and economic implications, ethics, future predictions, and sector-specific discussions like healthcare, cybersecurity, environment, entertainment, job market, and more. These insights comprehensively picture AI's pervasive impact in every facet of life.

Chapter 27 - 40: AI's Role in Various Sectors

I expanded our exploration to include various other sectors where AI leaves its mark. This included retail, real estate, manufacturing, tourism, journalism, language, food, fashion, archaeology, music, religion, gaming, insurance, human body augmentation, animal behavior studies, and more. Each sector presented unique applications, challenges, and implications of AI.

Afterword: The ABCs of AI - A Recap and Reflection

As our detailed exploration neared its end, I took a step back to reflect on the journey, revisiting the ABCs of AI and contemplating the transformative potential of AI and its implications for the future of our world. It was a pause that brought clarity and consolidation and evoked existential questions and concerns raised by AI.

Conclusion: Living with AI - Adapting to a New Normal

Finally, I concluded our journey with a call to action: embracing the AI revolution and understanding the importance of engaging with AI. I highlighted the role of individuals, governments, and organizations in shaping AI's future and reflected on the pervasive impact of AI on society. As we look forward to a world increasingly driven by AI, I underscore the need for adaptation, responsible AI use, and advocacy.

Glossary: Understanding AI Jargon

Our journey through the labyrinth of AI would not have been complete without a key to decipher its complex terminology.

The glossary was a handy reference guide to understanding AI jargon, ensuring the journey was as accessible as it was enlightening. This odyssey has unveiled the intricate tapestry of AI - its roots, mechanics, impact, potential, and the questions it provokes. The pervasive influence of AI underscores the importance of engaging with it, not just as a revolutionary technology but as a transformative force reshaping the contours of human life. As we conclude this comprehensive exploration, it is evident that our AI journey has just begun. As AI continues to evolve, so will our understanding and engagement. Our collective responsibility in this AI-driven future is to continually learn, adapt, and advocate for responsible AI use that benefits humanity at large.

SO, WE BEGIN!